WEIGHT TRAINING

Steps to Success

Second Edition

Thomas R. Baechle, EdD, CSCS, NSCA-CPT
Creighton University
Omaha, Nebraska

Barney R. Groves, PhD, CSCS
Virginia Commonwealth University
Richmond, Virginia

Human Kinetics

Library of Congress Cataloging-in-Publication Data

Baechle, Thomas R., 1943-
    Weight training : steps to success / Thomas R. Baechle, Barney R.
Groves. -- 2nd ed.
        p.   cm. -- (Steps to success activity series)
    Includes bibliographical references (p.).
    ISBN 0-88011-718-4
    1. Weight training.   I. Groves, Barney R., 1936-   .   II. Title.
III. Series.
GV546.3.B34   1998
613.7'13--dc21   97-44075
                                                                                 CIP

ISBN: 0-88011-718-4

Developmental Editor: Judy Patterson Wright, PhD; **Managing Editor:** Jacqueline Eaton Blakley; **Assistant Editors:** Erin Cler and Jennifer Stallard; **Editorial Assistant:** Jennifer Hemphill; **Copyeditor:** Jim Burns; **Proofreader:** Erin Cler; **Grapic Designer:** Keith Blomberg; **Graphic Artist:** Tara Welsch; **Cover Designer:** Jack Davis; **Photographer (cover):** Human Kinetics/Tom Roberts; **Illustrators:** Keith Blomberg and Jennifer Delmotte; **Printer:** United Grapics

Instructional Designer for the Steps to Success Activity Series: Joan N. Vickers, EdD, University of Calgary, Calgary, Alberta, Canada

Human Kinetics books are available at special discounts for bulk purchase. Special editions or book excerpts can also be created to specification. For details, contact the Special Sales Manager at Human Kinetics.

Printed in the United States of America   10   9   8   7   6   5   4   3   2   1

Human Kinetics
Web site: http://www.humankinetics.com/

United States: Human Kinetics, P.O. Box 5076, Champaign, IL 61825-5076
1-800-747-4457
e-mail: humank@hkusa.com

Canada: Human Kinetics, Box 24040, Windsor, ON N8Y 4Y9
1-800-465-7301 (in Canada only)
e-mail: humank@hkcanada.com

Europe: Human Kinetics, P.O. Box IW14, Leeds LS16 6TR, United Kingdom
(44) 1132 781708
e-mail: humank@hkeurope.com

Australia: Human Kinetics, 57A Price Avenue, Lower Mitcham, South Australia 5062
(088) 277 1555
e-mail: humank@hkaustralia.com

New Zealand: Human Kinetics, P.O. Box 105-231, Auckland 1
(09) 523 3462
e-mail: humank@hknewz.com

C ONTENTS

PREFACE

Recent research by sporting goods manufacturers acknowledges that weight training, with almost 40 million followers, is the single most popular type of fitness training activity in America. The reason for this popularity is quite simple. The results are quick, and they dramatically contribute to improved strength, muscle tone, body reproportioning, appearance, and health. Unfortunately, there aren't very many books on the subject that an inexperienced person can use with confidence. Terminology is often confusing, explanations are not clear, and readers are expected to assimilate too much information at one time. The approach taken in this book does not assume that one explanation or illustration is sufficient for becoming skilled at and knowledgeable about weight training. Instead, carefully developed procedures and drills accompany each step and provide ample practice and self-assessment opportunities.

This book focuses on two primary areas. One helps you to learn weight training exercises that are used within a well-balanced training program, and the other provides the knowledge needed to design weight training programs. The text begins by describing the manner in which your body will respond to weight training, the equipment that you will use, and dietary and training information that will be essential to your success. From this basis of understanding, basic lifting techniques and exercises are introduced; exercise techniques that are more complex follow this introduction. Recommended training loads are light while you are learning the exercises, and progress to heavier loads—loads that will bring about exciting results! Organizing exercises and loads in this manner also offers the best opportunity to learn exercises quickly and without fear of injury.

Once you have gained confidence in training, you are ready to learn how to design your own weight training program. The step-by-step explanations and self-assessment activities presented in Steps 11 and 12 make this the easiest of all weight training texts to follow and understand.

You will find that the use of practice procedures, drills, and self-assessment activities is also unique and is an effective approach to explaining the content and skills of weight training that is long overdue. This new edition also includes updated references, some different exercises (Appendix A), and variations to the previous practice and learning activities, making them more streamlined and easier to use. The new exercises that have been added require a higher level of skill, making this text more than a "beginner's text."

Also, since the publication of the first edition of *Weight Training: Steps to Success*, a video has been produced that clearly illustrates all of the exercises included in Steps 3 through 8 in this text, and also covers safety issues. This is an invaluable resource if you are trying to learn the exercises on your own or helping others to learn weight training exercises. Another excellent resource for instructors and personal trainers is the *Weight Training Instruction: Steps to Success* that has also been published since the first edition of this text. Written specifically for instructors, it provides the most comprehensive and helpful approach to teaching weight training on the market today. It includes ways to approach the strength assessment of students, information on assigning workout loads, strategies for teaching exercises, and sample lectures on designing training programs. *Weight Training Instruction: Steps to Success* in many ways mirrors the approach taken in this text and highlights the instructor's steps to success for teaching an introductory weight training class.

We would like to thank several people who directly or indirectly have influenced the development and completion of this book. Of special note is Dan Wathen, L/AT., C, whose contributions over the years have added much to our knowledge of weight training and to our personal lives. In addition, we thank Rich Coppins for help with the illustrations and Armetta Wright and Linda Tranisi for typing assistance. Most important have been our families, who have provided us with the motivation and support needed to complete this text. We would also like to recognize the artistic talents of Keith Blomberg, the graphic artist, and the support and direction provided by Judy Patterson Wright, our developmental editor.

STEPS TO SUCCESS STAIRCASE

Get ready to climb a staircase—one that will lead you to become stronger, more fit, and knowledgeable about weight training. You cannot leap to the top; you get there by climbing one step at a time.

Each of the 12 steps you will take is an easy transition from the one before it. The first few steps of the staircase provide a foundation—a solid foundation of basic skills and concepts. As you progress further, you will learn to complete a basic training program in a safe and time-efficient manner. You will also learn when and how to make needed changes in program intensity. As you near the top of the staircase, the climb eases and you'll find that you have developed a sense of confidence in your weight training skills and knowledge of how to design your own program. Perhaps most important, you will be pleased with how your body and fitness level are improving.

To understand how to build your training around the steps, familiarize yourself with the concepts and directions presented in the next sections. They provide information that will help you gain insights and an appreciation for weight training's tremendous popularity today, a knowledge of how your body reacts and adapts to training, and the importance of proper nutrition. Questions that you may have about machine and free weight equipment are also answered. Last, and perhaps most important, is the discussion regarding the essentials for training successfully. These "essentials" provide you with an understanding of key training concepts that will make every minute you spend in training count.

Approach each of the steps (chapters) that follow this first section in this way:

1. Read the explanation of what is covered in the step, why the step is important, and how to execute or perform the step's focus, which may be a basic skill, concept, approach, or combination of them.

2. Follow the Keys to Success illustrations showing exactly how to position your body to execute each exercise correctly. There are three general parts to each exercise. One is a preparation phase in which the techniques of getting into position are performed. The other two are execution phases, usually involving the performance of the upward and downward movements of an exercise. Note that whenever a movement phase includes a solid arrow tip (see Figure 1.6c), you should exhale (during the more difficult portion of the exercise). Conversely, whenever a hollow arrow tip is shown (see Figure 1.7a), you should inhale (during the easy portion of the exercise). For each large muscle group exercise in the basic program, you may select one exercise from three choices: a free weight exercise and two machine exercises.

3. Look over the descriptions in the "Success Stoppers" section for common errors that may occur and the recommendations for how to correct them.

4. The practice procedures and drills help you improve your skills through repetition and purposeful practice. Read the directions and the Success Goals for each drill and quiz.

Practice accordingly and record your score. Compare your performance with the Success Goal for the drill or self-assessment quiz. You need to meet the Success Goal of each drill or quiz before moving on to practice the next one because the drills progress from easy to difficult. The Success Checks that follow Success Goals provide additional insight about how to meet each goal. This sequence is designed specifically to help you achieve continual success.

5. As soon as you select all exercises in the basic program, you are ready to complete your first workout chart, make needed workout changes, and follow the basic program for minimum of 6 weeks. This is the time to evaluate your technique against the Keys to Success checklist.

6. Steps 10 and 11 prepare you to design your own program in Step 12. There are many helpful instructions, examples, and self-assessment opportunities (answers included) that will prepare you for the challenge. For example, formulas are provided to assist you in the difficult task of determining initial training loads and making needed adjustments to them.

7. Use the information in the appendices to either add to or replace exercises within the basic program (see Appendix A), to locate specific muscles (see Appendix B), and to chart your workout progress (see Appendix C).

Good luck on your step-by-step journey toward developing a strong, healthy, attractive body—a journey that will be confidence-building, rich in successes, and fun!

THE RENAISSANCE IN WEIGHT TRAINING

D emonstrations of strength have captured people's interest and imagination as far back as ancient times, but the merits of activities designed to develop strength have not always been well understood or appreciated. For many years it was believed that training with weights provided few if any benefits and, in fact, would reduce flexibility and impair neuromuscular coordination. A special concern was that training with weights would result in tremendous increases in muscular size. This was a primary concern among women, many of whom had been led to believe that having a strong-looking physique, or being strong, was unfeminine. These myths kept many from enjoying the benefits of weight training. Finally, in the 1930s two physical therapists, DeLorme and Wadkins, reported successful results using weight training in the rehabilitation of soldiers' arm and leg injuries. This began a "renaissance" in attitudes that sparked the evolution of weight training as we know it today.

Definitions and Myths

The term *weight training*, also referred to by many as *strength training*, pertains to the use of barbells, dumbbells, machines, and other equipment (weighted vests, bats, elastic tubing, and so on) for the purpose of improving fitness, appearance, and/or sports performance. The increasing popularity of weight training prompted researchers to study its effects, resulting in the discovery that many myths associated with weight training (e.g., that it reduces speed and causes "muscle-boundness") were unfounded. As the concerns about muscle *hypertrophy* (muscle size increase) and losses in speed, flexibility, and coordination dwindled, the benefits of increased *strength* (the ability to exert maximum force in a single effort), increased *muscular endurance* (the ability of a muscle to contract for an extended period of time without undue fatigue), and improved fitness became more apparent.

Along with the dispelling of the myths and a more universal use of weights among athletes and the general public came the growth of companies producing weight training equipment. Their design and marketing strategies created a different image of weight training. Sophisticated, attractive machines and chrome barbells and dumbbells replaced the rusty barbells and dumbbells typically found in less-than-aesthetically-pleasing surroundings. These changes made weight training not only an acceptable activity, but a trend-setting one among well-respected business people.

Weight Training Today

Impetus for weight training's current popularity also came from those interested in competitive weightlifting, power lifting, and body building. Competitive weightlifters perform "quick lifts" (snatch, and clean and jerk), whereas power lifters perform slower-moving lifts (squat, bench press, deadlift). Perhaps more popular, especially among women, is competitive body building, in which contestants are judged on muscular size, symmetry (muscular balance), general impression (appearance, mannerisms, etc.), and posing skill.

The 40+ million people who are weight training on a regular basis now see it as an effective method for improving health status, reproportioning and sculpting their bodies, and improving performance in sports and everyday activities requiring physical strength. Even the number of individuals involved in competitive aspects of weight training, especially power lifting and body building, is growing. On the other end of the spectrum, weight training is also growing in popularity among older populations, including individuals with osteoporosis and patients in cardiac rehabilitation programs.

There is little doubt that weight training has gained universal acceptance as an expedient method of improving the health, performance, and appearance of millions. The mythology surrounding weight training's Dark Ages has given way to mounting scientific evidence encouraging its use and an enlightened understanding of its benefits. A longtime advocate of and "key player" in creating this interest in and support for weight training has been the National Strength and Conditioning Association (NSCA). A nonprofit educational association of over 13,000 members from more than 65 countries, it stands alone as the world's recognized clearinghouse for accurate and up-to-date weight/strength training information. Their publication, *Essentials of Strength Training and Conditioning*, remains the most comprehensive text on strength training in the world. For information about the NSCA or this publication, call 719-632-6722 (fax 719-632-6367; e-mail nsca@usa.net) or write to NSCA at 530 Communications Circle, Suite 204, Colorado Springs, CO 80905.

PHYSIOLOGICAL CONSIDERATIONS

When weight training occurs on a regular basis and is accompanied by sensible eating choices, various systems of the body change in positive ways. Muscles become stronger, better toned, and show less fatigue with each additional session of training. The neuromuscular (nerve-muscle) system learns to work in better harmony. That is, the brain learns to selectively recruit specific muscles, and types of muscle fibers within them to assume the various loads used in your weight training exercises. The neuromuscular system also improves in its ability to control the speed of movement and to guide you through the correct movement patterns required in different exercises. This next section will help you to gain a better understanding of how your body responds physiologically to weight training, and to learn more about your nutritional needs, weight gain/loss issues, the importance of rest, and equipment and safety concerns.

Muscle Structure

On the basis of structure and function, muscle tissue is categorized into three types: *smooth*, *skeletal*, and *cardiac* (see Figure 1). In an activity such as weight training, the development of skeletal muscles is of paramount importance. As shown in Figure 2, skeletal muscles, sometimes referred to as *striated* muscles, are attached to the bone via tendon. Skeletal muscles respond to voluntary stimulation from the brain.

Although skeletal muscles (of which there are about 400) are grouped together, they function either separately or in concert with others. Which, and how many, skeletal muscles become involved in a workout depends upon which exercises are selected and the techniques used during their execution (e.g., width of grip or stance, angle and path that the bar is pushed or pulled—all have an effect on which muscles are recruited and to what extent). Illustrations and explanations of the muscle groups that are worked when performing many different exercises are located throughout this text. For example, Figure 3 shows the muscle, tendon, and bone relationship for the biceps muscle.

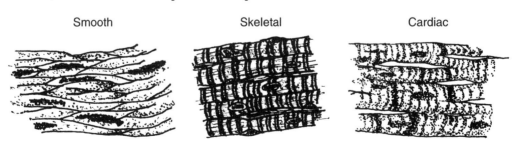

Smooth   Skeletal   Cardiac

Figure 1 Three types of muscle tissue.

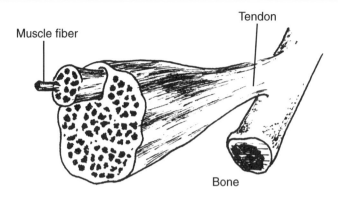

Figure 2 Tendons attach skeletal muscles to bones.

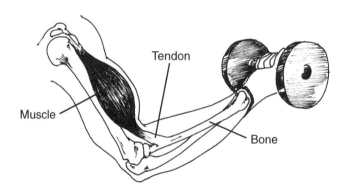

Figure 3 The biceps brachii muscle converges into a tendon and attaches to the radius bone in the forearm.

Types of Muscle Action

Isometric, *concentric*, and *eccentric* are the three different types of muscle action that can occur while weight training.

Isometric

The term *isometric*, or static, refers to situations in which tension develops in a muscle but no observable shortening or lengthening occurs. Sometimes during the execution of a repetition, a sticking point is reached, and there is a momentary pause in movement. The action of the muscle(s) at this point would be described as being static. Perhaps a more understandable example would be of a person attempting to push a bar off his or her chest (as in the bench press) when the load is too great to allow any movement upward.

Concentric

Concentric muscle action occurs when tension develops in a muscle, and the muscle shortens. For example, when the biceps muscles move the barbell toward the shoulders in the dumbbell curl shown in Figure 4a, the muscles' action is described as concentric. Another example is when the abdominal muscles shorten to flex the trunk forward in the sit-up exercise. The work that muscles perform during concentric activity is also referred to as "positive work."

Eccentric

The term *eccentric* is used to describe muscle action in which tension is present in the muscle, but the muscle lengthens instead of shortens. Using the biceps curl as an example again, once the dumbbell begins the lowering phase in Figure 4b the eccentric action of the biceps controls the descent of the dumbbell. There still is tension in the biceps muscles; the difference (as compared to the concentric) is that the muscle fibers slowly lengthen to control the rate of lowering of the dumbbell. Using the example of the sit-up described earlier, the controlled lowering of the trunk back to the mat is accomplished by the eccentric activity of the abdominal muscles. This is referred to as "negative work," because it is being performed in the direction opposite to that of the concentric (positive). It is the eccentric (lengthening) action, versus concentric (shortening), that is primarily responsible for the muscle soreness associated with weight training.

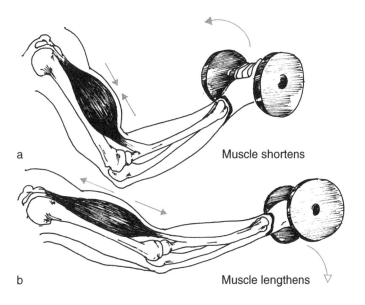

a

Muscle shortens

b

Muscle lengthens

Figure 4 Concentric biceps curl (a) and eccentric biceps curl (b).

Factors Affecting Strength Gains

The strength that you are able to develop from weight training is influenced by neuromuscular changes (referred to as "neural" hereafter) that occur through the process of learning exercises, increasing muscle mass, and your fiber type composition.

Strength Defined

The term *strength* refers to the ability to exert maximum force during a single effort. It can be measured by determining a 1-repetition maximum effort, referred to as a "1RM," in one or more exercises. For example, if you loaded a bar to 100 pounds and were able to complete (using a maximum effort) only 1 repetition (rep), your 1RM equals 100 pounds. Strength is specific to a muscle or muscle area (this specificity concept will be discussed later).

Neural Changes

Two reasons have been accepted to explain the strength increases that occur in response to weight training. One is associated with neural changes, and the other involves increases in muscle mass. In the first case, the term "neural" refers to the nervous system working with the muscular system to increase strength. In doing so, the nerves that are attached to specific muscle fibers are "taught" when to "transmit." Thus, an improvement in the lifting technique occurs that permits handling poundages more efficiently (with less effort).

Furthermore, through repetition your body becomes able to recruit more fibers, and to selectively recruit those fibers that are most effective in "getting the job done." Thus, there is a learning factor that contributes to strength changes, some of which may be quite dramatic. It is well accepted that this neural-learning factor accounts for the strength improvements seen during the first weeks of weight training.

Muscle Mass Changes

Although the neural-learning factor continues to play a role, continued gains in strength are mostly associated with increases in muscle mass. As the cross-sectional area of the muscle becomes greater (because the individual fibers become thicker and stronger), so does the muscle's ability to exert force. Therefore, the neural factor accounts for the early increases in strength, whereas muscle mass increases are responsible for the changes seen later.

Strength Increases—What to Expect

Depending on training habits and level of strength at the time of initial testing, the muscle group being evaluated, the intensity of the training program (loads, repetitions, sets, rest periods), the length of the training program (weeks, months, years), and genetic potential, reported strength increases typically range from 8 percent to 50 percent. The greatest improvements are seen among those who have not weight trained before and in programs involving large-muscle exercises, heavier loads, multiple sets, and more training sessions. Unique characteristics, such as the lengths of muscles and the angles at which their tendons insert onto the bone, provide mechanical advantages and disadvantages and are factors that also increase or limit your strength potential. The effects of steroid use on strength and muscle mass will be discussed later.

Gender Differences

It should not be a surprise to hear that men are typically stronger than women. However, it has nothing to do with the *quality* of muscle tissue or its ability to produce force, since these are identical in both sexes. The *quantity* of muscle tissue in the average male (40 percent) versus female (23 percent) is largely responsible for men's strength superiority. It is this difference that also helps to explain why women typically are 43 percent to 63 percent weaker in upper body strength, and 25 percent to 30 percent weaker in lower body strength.

To conclude from this, however, that women do not have the same potential as men to gain strength is entirely incorrect. A female can develop strength relative to her own potential, but it will not be at the absolute strength levels achieved by males. Furthermore, weight training research studies repeatedly show that women can make dramatic improvements in strength and muscle tone without fear of developing unwanted muscle bulk and can decrease body fat at the same time, resulting in a healthier and more attractive appearance.

When to Expect Strength Changes

The strength improvements that occur in response to weight training are not typically noticeable until the third or fourth week of training. The first week is usually characterized by losses in strength, perhaps due to the microtrauma (tearing down) of muscle tissue. Fatigue may also be a contributing factor. Decreases in strength performance are especially apparent during the final training session of the first week, so do not be surprised if you feel weaker toward the end of that week. Of course, in the weeks ahead you will be impressed and excited about the strength improvements, which may be as great as 4 percent to 6 percent per week.

Why Muscles Increase in Size

Exactly what accounts for muscle-size increases is not fully understood; however, factors that are often discussed are hypertrophy, hyperplasia, and genetic potential.

Hypertrophy

Muscle-size increases are most often attributed to an enlargement of existing fibers, the same fibers that are present at birth. Very thin protein myofibrils (actin and myosin) within the fiber increase in size, creating a larger fiber. The collective effect of increases within many individual fibers is responsible for the overall muscle-size changes observed. This increase in existing fibers is referred to as hypertrophy (Figure 5).

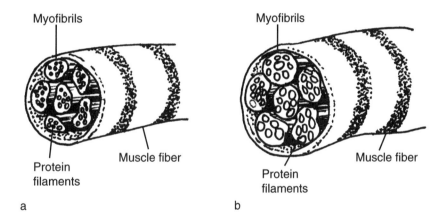

Figure 5 Muscle hypertrophy: the muscle before training (a) and the muscle after training (b). Note the changes in the diameters of the protein filaments that constitute the myofibrils.

Hyperplasia

Although hypertrophy is the most commonly accepted explanation of why a muscle becomes larger, there are studies suggesting that fibers split lengthwise and form separate fibers. The splitting is thought to contribute to an increase in the size of the muscle. This theory of longitudinal fiber splitting is referred to as hyperplasia.

Muscle Fiber Type and Genetic Potential

If one accepts hypertrophy as the process whereby existing fibers increase in size, then one must also accept the idea that there are genetic limitations regarding the extent to which muscle will increase in size. This is because increases are due to the thickening of fibers that already exist. Just as we know that some people are born with muscle-tendon attachments favoring force development, the same is true in regard to the number of muscle fibers. Some people are born with a greater number of muscle fibers than others, and therefore their genetic potential for muscle-size growth is greater. Regardless of your genetic inheritance, your challenge is to design an effective program of training and to train diligently so that you develop to your full potential.

The skeletal muscle tissue mentioned earlier can be categorized into two basic types, each with unique capabilities and characteristics. *Fast-twitch* muscle fiber has the capacity to produce a great deal of force but fatigues quickly. Typically its size will also increase more rapidly. Fast-twitch fibers, because of their high force capability, are recruited during weight training exercises and in athletic events requiring high levels of explosive strength (e.g., shot put, discus, javelin, football). *Slow-twitch* muscle fiber is not able to exert as much force or to develop force as quickly but is more enduring—that is, it can continue contracting for longer periods of time before fatigue occurs. Slow-twitch fibers are recruited for aerobic-oriented events (e.g., distance running, swimming, biking) that have lower strength but greater endurance requirements.

Not everyone possesses the same proportion of fast-twitch to slow-twitch muscle fibers. Individuals who possess a greater number of fast-twitch fibers have a greater genetic potential to be stronger and, therefore, to be more successful in certain "strength-dependent" sports or in activities like weight training. Conversely, individuals with a higher percentage of slow-twitch fibers have greater genetic potential to be successful in events requiring lower levels of strength and greater levels of endurance, such as long-distance swimming or marathoning events.

Muscular Endurance Improvements

Muscular endurance refers to the muscle's ability to perform repeatedly with moderate loads for an extended period of time. Improvement in your muscular endurance is demonstrated by an ability to extend the period of time before muscular fatigue occurs, e.g., perform more repetitions. Thus, it is different from strength, the measure of a single, "all-out" muscular effort. But like strength, muscular endurance is specific to the muscle or muscles involved. For instance, as a result of regularly performing a high number of reps in the biceps curl, muscles in the front of the upper arm will improve in their endurance. But this training will not improve muscular endurance in the leg muscles.

Weight training appears to bring about muscular endurance improvements in two ways: by increasing anaerobic qualities in the muscle, and by reducing the number of muscle fibers involved during earlier periods of an activity, thereby leaving some in reserve should the activity continue. The reduction in the number of fibers involved is related to strength improvements that permit a task to be undertaken using a lower percentage of effort. For example, if you had to perform a 25-pound biceps curl and had 50 pounds of strength in your biceps, this exercise would require 50 percent of your strength. If, however, your biceps strength increased to 100 pounds, the task would now require only 25 percent of your strength. Thus, a lower percentage of effort would be required to perform a biceps curl with 25 pounds.

Cardiovascular Fitness Improvements

The effects of weight training on cardiovascular fitness, typically expressed as changes in oxygen uptake (the ability to transport and utilize oxygen by the muscles), have been studied by numerous researchers. It is safe to say that weight training programs involving heavier loads, fewer repetitions, and longer rest periods between sets have a minimal effect on cardiovascular fitness. However, when weight training programs include light to moderate loads (40 to 60 percent of 1RM), a greater number of repetitions (12 to 20+), and very short rest periods between sets (30 to 60 seconds), moderate (5 percent) improvements in oxygen uptake may be expected. The extent of such changes is also influenced by the intensity and length of the overall training period (weeks, months, years) as well as fitness and strength levels at the start of a training program. It would be an oversight to disregard these considerations when evaluating the merits of reported cardiovascular fitness improvements attributed to weight training programs.

The most effective way to develop cardiovascular fitness is to engage in aerobic training activities such as walking, running, swimming, cycling, or cross-country skiing. Such activities involve continuous, rhythmic movements that can be sustained for longer periods of time than anaerobic activities such as weight training. Guidelines that will help you develop an aerobic exercise program can be found in the texts by Baechle and Earle (1995), Corbin and Lindsey (1997), Hoeger (1995), and Westcott and Baechle (1998) listed in the references section at the end of this text. A well-designed fitness program will include both weight training and aerobic activities.

Muscular Coordination and Flexibility Improvements

Some people still believe that weight training will somehow negatively affect muscular coordination and reduce flexibility. The heaviness in the arms and legs and the numb feeling (loss of "touch") that occurs immediately after a set of repetitions are only temporary and will not reduce coordination levels. Weight training sessions most likely will have the opposite effect. Handling and moving bars from the floor to overhead (standing press), balancing the bar on your back (back squat), and evenly pressing dumbbells (dumbbell flys) all contribute to improving muscular coordination.

Weight training exercises performed using good technique and in a controlled manner can improve strength throughout all ranges of joint motion. Exercises performed in this way will improve flexibility as well as provide a better stimulus for strength development, and they may reduce the likelihood of injury. There is no reliable evidence to support the contention that properly performed weight training exercises reduce flexibility or motor coordination!

Delayed Muscular Soreness

You should not be surprised or discouraged to find that the first week or two of weight training is accompanied by extreme muscle soreness. It is natural to feel as if 300 of your approximately 400 muscles have been stung rather than exercised. Muscle soreness, in varying degrees, is experienced by virtually all who weight train. There is no definitive explanation of why we experience delayed muscle soreness, but it is known that the eccentric (or "negative") phase of exercise movements produces it. As an example, the lowering (eccentric) phases of the biceps curl and bench press result in muscle soreness, but the upward (concentric) phases do not. Usually the discomfort of muscle soreness subsides after 3 days, especially if you stretch before and after training. Surprisingly, the very thing that stimulates the soreness (i.e., exercise) helps to alleviate it. Light exercise combined with stretching activities is ideal for speeding the recovery from muscle soreness.

Avoid Overtraining

Overtraining is a condition in which there is a plateau or drop in performance over a period of time. This occurs when your body does not have time to adequately recuperate from training before the next workout. Often the overtrained state is a result of overlooking the need to rest between sessions, working out too aggressively (especially too soon after illness) including too many training sessions per week, or not following recommended program guidelines presented in this text.

Warning Signs

The physical warning signs of overtraining are

1. extreme muscular soreness and stiffness the day after a training session;
2. a gradual increase in muscular soreness from one training session to the next;
3. a decrease in body weight (especially when no effort to decrease body weight is being made);
4. an inability to complete a training session that, based upon your present physical condition, is reasonable; and
5. a decrease in appetite.

Prevention Strategies

If you develop two or more of the above symptoms, you should reduce the intensity, frequency, and/or duration of training until these warning signs abate. It is more desirable to prevent overtraining than to try to recover from it.

To help prevent overtraining:

- increase training intensity gradually;
- alternate aggressive with less aggressive training weeks, allowing for sufficient recovery between training sessions (discussed in Step 11);
- get adequate amounts of sleep;
- eat properly; and
- make adjustments in training intensity as needed.

NUTRITIONAL AND BODY WEIGHT ISSUES

Nutrition is basically the study of how carbohydrates, proteins, fats, vitamins, minerals, and water provide the energy, substances, and nutrients required for maintaining bodily functions during rest and exercise conditions. When a sound nutrition program is combined with regular training sessions, success is a natural outcome. The general guidelines for a healthy diet—55 percent carbohydrates, 30 percent fats, and 15 percent proteins—are appropriate for those who are weight training. However, you may want to slightly increase the amount of carbohydrates and decrease the amount of fats. Try to select complex, instead of simple, carbohydrates and unsaturated, instead of saturated, fats. A diet that includes appropriate amounts of fluids (six to eight glasses) and is selected with these diet guidelines in mind will provide the necessary energy and nutrients to promote positive changes in your strength, endurance, and muscularity.

Nutritional Needs

The discussion that follows is an overview of the nutritional and dietary factors that will affect the manner in which your body responds to your dietary and training habits. For more information on this topic refer to *Nancy Clark's Sports Nutrition Guidebook*, 2nd edition (1997).

Carbohydrates

Carbohydrates are the body's primary source of energy. They provide 4 kilocalories per gram and are categorized as either complex or simple. For those who train intensely, an increased intake of complex carbohydrates is very important. Preferred sources of carbohydrates include cereals, breads, flours, grains, fruits, pasta, and vegetables (complex carbohydrates). Other sources are syrups, jellies, cakes, and honey (simple carbohydrates).

Fats

Fats provide a concentrated form of energy (9 kilocalories per gram)—more than twice that of carbohydrates or proteins. Fats are involved in the maintenance of healthy skin, insulation against heat and cold, and protection of vital organs, and are the major storage form of energy. Fats can be found in both plant and animal sources, and are usually classified as saturated or unsaturated. Unsaturated fats (mono and poly), such as those found in olive, canola, and corn oil, are preferred because they are associated with a lower risk of developing heart disease. Common sources of saturated fat include meats such as beef, lamb, chicken, and pork. Other sources are dairy products, such as cream, milk, cheese, and butter, and egg yolks.

Proteins

Proteins are the building blocks of all body cells. They are responsible for the repair, rebuilding, and replacement of cells as well as for regulating bodily processes involved in fighting infection. If the supply of carbohydrates and fats is insufficient and the responsibility of repairing, rebuilding, and regulating metabolic functions has been met, protein is used as a source of energy. Proteins provide 4 kilocalories per gram. The basic units of protein are the amino acids, which are in turn further described as essential or nonessential amino acids. Of the 20 amino acids, 8 (or 9, depending on what reference is consulted) are termed essential amino acids and must be supplied through the diet. The other 12 (or 11) can be produced by the body; these are the nonessential amino acids. Foods that contain all of the essential amino acids are called complete proteins. Meat, fish, poultry, eggs, milk, and cheese are sources of complete proteins. Suggested protein sources that are low in fat include milk products, lean meats, and fish. Incomplete sources of protein include breads, cereals, nuts, dried peas, and beans.

Vitamins

Vitamins are essential nutrients needed for many body processes. They are divided into two types, fat soluble and water soluble. Regardless of the type, vitamins do not contain energy or calories, and extra vitamin supplementation will not provide more energy.

Minerals

Minerals function in the body as builders, activators, regulators, transmitters, and controllers of the body's metabolic processes. Like vitamins, minerals do not provide calories.

Water

While not a provider of energy for activity, water provides the medium for, and is one of, the end products of activity. Water makes up about 72 percent of the weight of muscle and represents 40 to 60 percent of an individual's total body weight. Through the regulation of thirst and urine output the body is able to keep a delicate water balance. When an appropriate balance is not maintained, the body's ability to function normally is compromised.

The Food Guide Pyramid

The Food Guide Pyramid, developed by the USDA and the Department of Health and Human Services, can help you choose the best foods for a healthy diet (see Figure 6). It is recommended that you eat a variety of foods to get the nutrients you need, and to increase the amount of breads, fruits, and vegetables in your diet while reducing the amount of fats and added sugars.

The Diet Dilemma and Weight Loss

Body composition considers the amount of fat weight and fat-free (muscle, bone, organ) weight that makes up your body. This is in contrast to judging physical makeup solely on what the weight scale registers as your body weight, as shown in Figure 7. Thus, body composition is a more accurate way to describe your health and fitness status. Two factors that have a profound effect on body composition are diet and exercise.

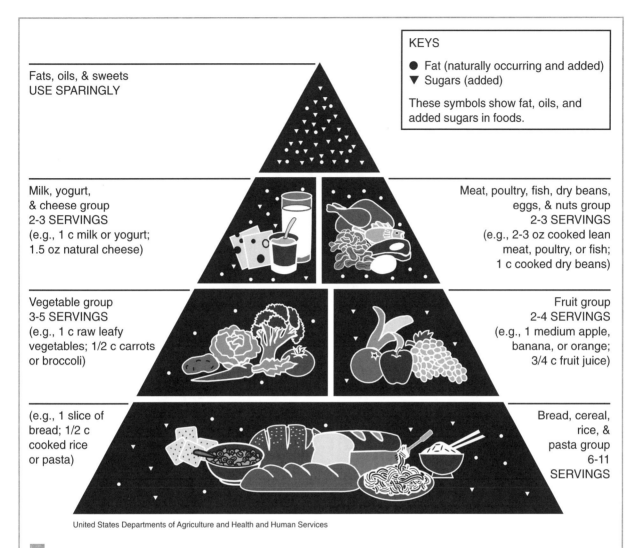

Fats, oils, & sweets
USE SPARINGLY

KEYS

● Fat (naturally occurring and added)
▼ Sugars (added)

These symbols show fat, oils, and added sugars in foods.

Milk, yogurt,
& cheese group
2-3 SERVINGS
(e.g., 1 c milk or yogurt;
1.5 oz natural cheese)

Meat, poultry, fish, dry beans,
eggs, & nuts group
2-3 SERVINGS
(e.g., 2-3 oz cooked lean
meat, poultry, or fish;
1 c cooked dry beans)

Vegetable group
3-5 SERVINGS
(e.g., 1 c raw leafy
vegetables; 1/2 c carrots
or broccoli)

Fruit group
2-4 SERVINGS
(e.g., 1 medium apple,
banana, or orange;
3/4 c fruit juice)

(e.g., 1 slice of
bread; 1/2 c
cooked rice
or pasta)

Bread, cereal,
rice, &
pasta group
6-11
SERVINGS

United States Departments of Agriculture and Health and Human Services

Figure 6 Food Guide Pyramid.

Unfortunately, approximately 65 million Americans are on some type of diet at any given time. Millions more are going on diets every day. Some are losing weight, but many are gaining it back. All hope to somehow find the answer. The truth is that the diets designed to create a fast weight loss typically are not effective in helping people stay healthy and trim; in fact, many of those diets are actually harmful.

Metabolic Rate Fluctuations

There are good reasons why diets typically don't work and better reasons why wise food selection plus regular exercise does work. Crash diets, in particular, are not effective because the body quickly adapts to a lower food intake by reducing its metabolic rate (i.e., the rate at which food is burned for energy). This compensatory action by the body resists the burning of fat. When there is a dietary restriction resulting in a loss of 10 pounds, for example, the body adjusts to the restricted diet. Later, when increased food intake occurs, even though daily consumption is still less than it was before dieting, the body treats the increase as excess and stores it as fat. This "yo-yo" cycle of losing weight and quickly gaining it back is not only ineffective in creating a positive body appearance, but also is unhealthy (as described later).

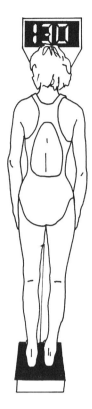
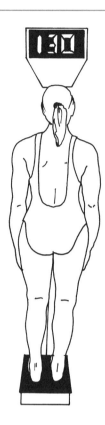

Figure 7 Comparison of two women with the same weight but different body compositions. Note that although the woman on the left weighs the same as the woman on the right, she is much leaner.

Fluctuations Due to Water Loss

You should realize that the weight loss experienced during the early part of a strict diet program is usually a loss of water, not fat. Many diets restrict carbohydrate intake. This reduces the water content of the body because much of the water stored in our bodies is accumulated in the process of storing carbohydrates. Weight loss due to the reduction of water stores is only temporary. Once the fluid balance is restored, the weight scale does not reflect the loss of body fat that was assumed to have occurred.

Muscle Tissue Loss

Also, if a female dieter consumes less than about 1,200 kilocalories a day (1,500 kilocalories a day for a male), muscle tissue as well as fat is usually lost. The farther the caloric intake dips below this amount, the more muscle tissue is lost compared to fat. So even though the dieter loses weight, he or she is actually fatter because the percentage of body fat compared to that of lean body weight has increased. The goal of a sound diet should be to reduce total body weight without losing muscle tissue. People who are on the roller coaster of dieting, gaining weight, and dieting again may be weakening their body every time they diet. This "yo-yo" approach is the wrong way to lose weight; it has a negative effect on the body, and it is ineffective for maintaining an appropriate level of body fat.

Body Size Considerations

It appears that many overweight people justify their overeating by thinking that because their bodies are heavy, they need more food to nourish them. Actually, the opposite is true in many cases. Too much of their body weight is fat, which, unlike muscle, is not as metabolically active. In contrast, exercising muscles burn calories; the more muscle there is, the more energy is expended and the faster stored fat is reduced. Compare two individuals who are the same height, one of whom weighs more and is in worse physical condition than the other. The lighter person has more muscle and less stored fat due to a good fitness level, and will require a greater caloric intake than the less active, heavier, fatter, and less muscular person.

Values of Weight Training and Aerobic Exercise

For many, the most effective way to decrease excess body fat is to moderately reduce caloric intake while participating in an aerobic and weight training program. These exercise programs will burn calories and maintain or build muscle tissue, which encourages an improvement in the fat-to-muscle ratio. In 40 minutes of aerobic exercise, the average individual burns approximately 400 to 480 kilocalories. Keep in mind that aerobic activities involve the large muscles in continuous activities such as in cycling, swimming, walking, jogging, cross-country skiing, and rope skipping. These activities promote the greatest caloric expenditure. Golf, on the other hand, is not a continuous and rhythmic activity and burns only half the calories that swimming the backstroke does for individuals of the same body weight.

Weight training sessions do not typically expend as many calories as aerobic exercise sessions, but they do maintain or increase muscle mass. This is important because by adding more muscle more calories are burned.

Losing Fat Weight

If you want to lose body fat, attempt to lose it at a maximum rate of 1 to 2 pounds per week. Losses greater than this result in losses of muscle tissue. A pound of fat has approximately 3,500 kilocalories, so a daily dietary reduction of 250 to 500 kilocalories will total about 1,750 to 3,500 kilocalories a week. Combined with regular exercise, this will promote the recommended loss of 1 to 2 pounds of fat per week and help keep it off.

Gaining Fat-Free Weight

Most people who exercise have no interest in gaining body weight; however, there are some who participate in weight training programs specifically to gain muscle. To accomplish this, there needs to be an increase in caloric consumption in combination with regular training. The weight training will stimulate muscle growth, and thus body weight increases. The consumption of additional calories (beyond one's daily needs) provides the basis for the increase in muscle tissue. The addition of 1 pound of muscle requires 2,500 kilocalories more than normal metabolic needs. An equal increase in proteins and carbohydrates (with a special emphasis on complex carbohydrates) and a maintenance of fat intake should help promote lean tissue growth and an increase in muscle size.

Note that a woman typically does not become as muscular as a man, so it is unlikely that she will significantly gain body weight in response to weight training unless she makes an effort to do so (by increasing food intake and following a program designed to develop hypertrophy).

Protein Needs, Supplements, and Steroids

Although protein, mineral, and vitamin supplementation is strongly endorsed by many, little research has been presented that substantiates claims of improved muscular endurance, hypertrophy, or strength among individuals who eat well. Again and again, dietitians, exercise physiologists, and sports medicine physicians conclude that a normal diet will meet protein dietary needs of the typical person. The exception may be that an increase in carbohydrate and protein intake is appropriate for those who participate in aggressive weight training programs.

Steroid Use Considerations

Conversations regarding supplementation are all too often accompanied by questions concerning steroids. It is human nature to look for shortcuts, and this is especially common among people who desire to make their body more attractive, stronger, and healthier. But there are no safe shortcuts. Anabolic-androgenic steroids in the presence of adequate diet and training can contribute to an increase in lean body mass; however, *the harmful side effects from anabolic steroid treatments greatly outweigh any positive effect.*

There are two forms of steroids: oral, or pill form; and water- or oil-based liquid that is injected using a hypodermic needle. These two forms are gauged for potency by comparing the anabolic effects (muscle-building and strength-inducing) versus the androgenic effects (increased male or female secondary sex characteristics such as increased body hair length or density, voice lowering, and breast enlargement). This ratio is termed the therapeutic index.

Adverse Side Effects

Studies included in a position paper by the National Strength and Conditioning Association on steroid use (Stone 1993) have cited increases in muscle size and strength, but not all outcomes from their use are that positive. Prolonged high dosages of steroids can lead to long lasting impairment of normal testosterone endocrine (natural steroid) function, and decreasing natural testosterone levels and potential for future physical development. With a decrease in testosterone the body cannot make gains or even retain what had already been developed.

The health consequences of steroid use can include chronic illness such as heart disease, liver trouble, urinary tract abnormalities, and sexual dysfunction. A shortened life may be a consequence. There are also immediate short-term effects, including increased blood pressure, acne, testicular atrophy, gynecomastia (male breast enlargement), sore nipples, decreased sperm count, prostatic enlargement, and increased aggression. Other side effects that have been reported include hair loss, fever, nausea, diarrhea, nosebleeds, lymph node swelling, increased appetite, and a burning sensation during urination. The major psychological symptoms include paranoia, delusions of grandeur, and auditory hallucinations.

When steroid use is discontinued after short-term use, most side effects disappear. However, females who take steroids may have permanent deepening of the voice, facial hair, baldness, clitoral enlargement, and a decrease in breast size.

One of the most serious effects of taking anabolic steroids is the increased probability of developing coronary artery disease. Users often have high levels of total cholesterol, low levels of the desirable high density lipoprotein (HDL) component, and elevated blood pressure, all of which are significant heart disease risk factors.

EQUIPMENT ORIENTATION

alking into a well-equipped weight room can be somewhat intimidating when you are new to weight training. As you look around, you will see machines of various sizes and shapes, short and long bars, and weight plates (that fit onto the bars) of different sizes/poundages with holes of different sizes. It can be confusing as well as intimidating. However, because the equipment that is available to you oftentimes dictates the exercises that you will be able to include in your workouts, becoming familiar with it is a logical first step in starting a weight training program. Also important is learning the "whys and hows" of equipment use that will help to avoid injury. This section will include information about the types, characteristics, and safe uses of machine and free weight training equipment.

Machine Equipment

Most machines in a workout facility are designed to accommodate what is referred to as a dynamic form of exercise—that is, exercises involving movement. In contrast are isometric exercises in which no observable movement occurs, such as pulling or pushing against a fixed bar. Dynamic exercises performed on weight machines typically challenge muscles to shorten against resistance and lengthen in a controlled manner while being "loaded" (see the "Physiological Considerations" section).

Fixed Resistance Equipment

Figure 8 shows two types of single-unit (a, b) and one type of multi-unit (c) machines. The single-unit pulley (a) and pivot arm (b) types of machines are designed to work primarily one muscle area. Multi-unit machines have various stations attached to their frame, allowing many muscle areas to be worked by simply moving from station to station.

A closer look at the structure of these machines reveals how they are designed. The weight stack in Figure 9a is lifted by pushing a weight arm attached to a fixed pivot point, and in Figure 9b the weight stack is lifted by pulling down on a handle affixed to a cable-pulley arrangement. Sometimes a chain, or flat belt is used in place of the cable shown in Figure 9b.

You will notice when using fixed resistance equipment that some movement phases require more effort than others, as though someone were changing the weight of the weight stack on you. Really what has happened is that as the weight arm moves in response to being pushed or pulled, it changes the location of the weight stack (WS) in relation to the weight arm's pivot point (PP). This is illustrated in Figure 10. As the distance between the weight stack and the pivot point becomes shorter, the exercise requires less effort, and as the distance between these two points becomes greater, the exercise requires more effort. If you are familiar with leverage concepts, you understand the specific reasons for all of this.

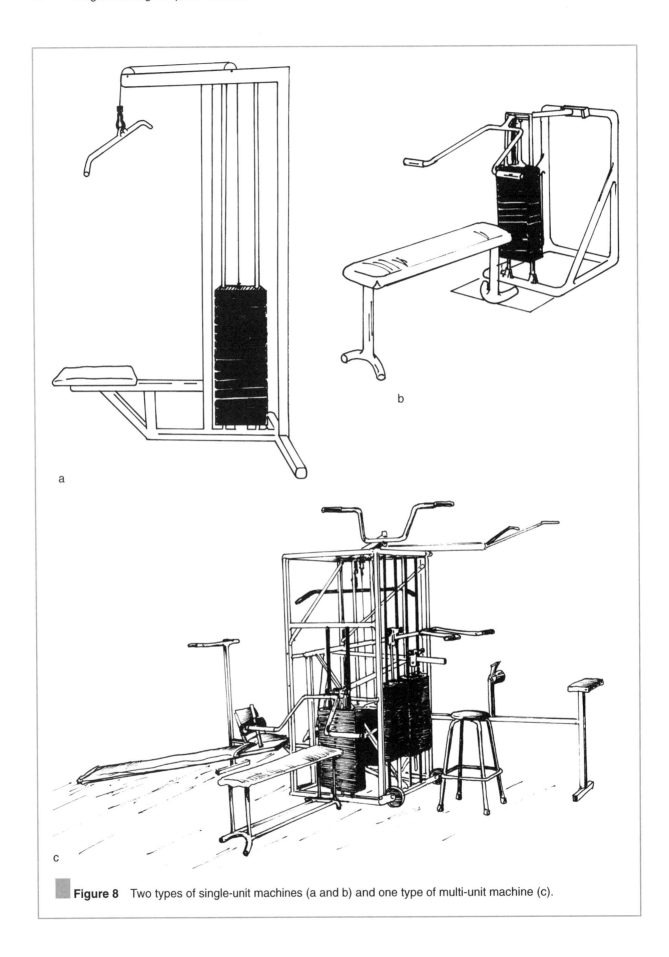

a

b

c

Figure 8 Two types of single-unit machines (a and b) and one type of multi-unit machine (c).

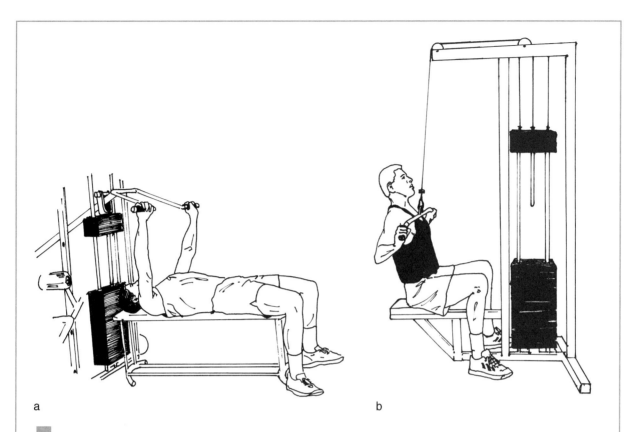

a

b

Figure 9 Structure of pivot arm bench press (a) and pulley-type lat pull-down machines (b).

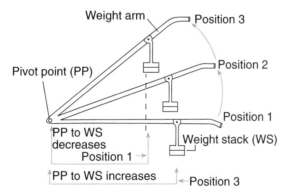

Figure 10 Fixed resistance machine function. Note that as the weight arm is moved from position 1 to position 3, the distance from the pivot point (PP) to the weight stack (WS) decreases, making the exercise easier to complete.

Machines that feature a fixed pivot or the circular-shaped pulley design are commonly referred to as *fixed resistance* machines. The limitation of this type of equipment is that the muscles are not taxed in a consistent manner throughout the exercise range. Free weights also fall into this category and present the same limitation.

Variable Resistance Equipment

In an effort to create a more consistent stress on muscles, some machines are designed to allow the weight stack to roll or slide back and forth on the weight arm of the machine (Figure 11a). These machines are referred to as *variable resistance machines*. Note again the relationship between the weight stack and the pivot point as the stack moves. When the weight arm moves to a position that would require less effort with a fixed pivot machine, the weight stack on the variable resistance machine moves away from the pivot point. When it is pushed or pulled to a position requiring more effort, the weight stack moves closer to the pivot point. The result of these changes are seen in Figure 11b. There is more to understanding why a more consistent stress is imposed throughout the entire range of an exercise with the moving pivot, but the explanation here is sufficient to help you recognize the capabilities of these variable resistance machines.

To create a more consistent stress, variable resistance machines may also feature a somewhat kidney-shaped wheel or cam. The effect of cam shape on weight stack location can be observed in Figures 12 a and b. As the chain (or cable or belt) tracks over the peaks and valleys of the cam, notice that the distance between the pivot point (the axle on which the

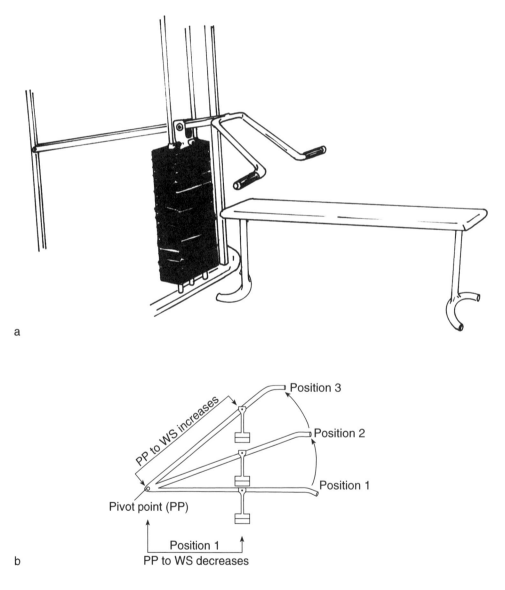

Figure 11 Variable resistance machine function. Note that as the weight arm is moved from position 1 to position 3, the distance from the pivot point (PP) to the weight stack (WS) increases, making the exercise harder to complete.

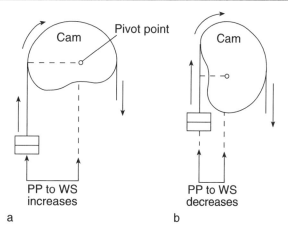

Figure 12 Variable resistance cam function (a and b). The cam functions similarly to the moving weight stack by varying the distance between the PP and the WS, thereby creating a more uniform stress on the muscles.

cam rotates) and the weight stack changes. This variation in distance from the pivot point to the location of the weight stack is what creates a more uniform loading on muscles. If you care to gain a better understanding of the principles involved in the equipment described here, consider reading Baechle (1995), Garhammer (1986), and Westcott and Baechle (1998).

Isokinetic Equipment

Not as common but also popular are isokinetic machines (Figure 13). These machines are designed so that exercises (dynamic) on them are performed at a constant speed. Unlike variable resistance machines that involve concentric and eccentric muscle actions, isokinetic equipment involves only concentric muscle activity. And instead of using weight stacks, these machines create resistance by using hydraulic, pneumatic, or frictional features. Control settings on these machines allow you to select movement speeds that relate to the level of resistance desired, going from slower speeds requiring greater effort to faster speeds that require less effort as you move through the range of the exercise movement.

Isokinetic machines provide a resistance to movement that is equivalent to the force you exert. The harder you push or pull, the greater will be the resistance you experience. The weaker the effort, the less the resistance. The primary difference between variable resistance and isokinetic machines is that with the former, the shape of the cam or the position of the roller dictates the effort you must exert. With isokinetic machines, how hard you push or pull determines the effort throughout the exercise movement.

Training Precautions With Machines

It is common to hear that weight training machines are safer to train on than free weights. It is true that they are *inherently* safer to use because the weight stacks are located away from the person lifting and the bars are suspended or stationary. Thus, it is less likely that dropped weight plates and bars will cause the kinds of injuries we sometimes see with free weights. The stationary nature of machines also permits safer travel to and from exercise stations (verses carrying a barbell or dumbbell). Another advantage is that if you intend to train on your own, you will not need a spotter.

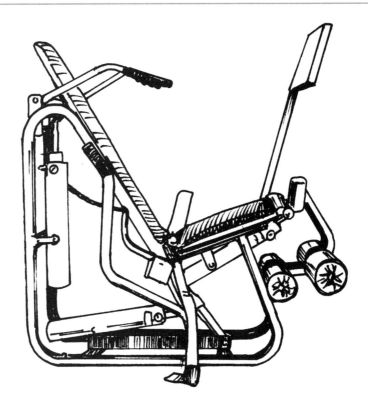

Figure 13 Isokinetic machine.

Even with these advantages of machines over free weights, injuries are more common on machines. This is probably because those who have limited experience in the weight room are less fearful of machines and will attempt to perform exercises on them without proper instruction. Doing so on machines can result in injury to muscles, tendons, and joint structures if momentum is not controlled by performing exercises in a *slow, controlled* manner.

Given that the use of machines can result in injury to muscles, tendons, and joint structures, there are several essential guidelines to follow that will make training on them more safe and productive: (1) position yourself into machines properly; (2) perform exercises using the techniques described; and (3) perform exercises in a slow, controlled manner. Additional precautions to take when preparing to train follow.

Before Using Machines

Before using machines, check for frayed cables and belts, worn pulleys and chains, broken welds, loose pads, and uneven or rough movement. If any of these exist, do not use machines until they have been repaired. Adjust levers and seats to accommodate your body size. Never place your fingers or hands between weight stacks to dislodge a selector key or to adjust loads, and keep them away from the chains, belts, pulleys, and cams.

When Using Machines

When you are training on machines, assume a stable position on the seats, pads, and rollers. Fasten seat belts securely. Choose an appropriate load. Insert selector keys all the way. Perform exercises through the full range of motion in a slow and controlled manner.

Do not allow the weight stacks to bounce during the lower phases of exercises or to hit the pulleys during the upward phases.

Free Weight Equipment

Free weight equipment is different in design and slightly different in function than its machine counterpart. The term "free" refers to its nonrestrictive effect on joint movement, which is in contrast to machines that create a predetermined movement pattern. It is this characteristic that enables you to perform so many different exercises with only one barbell or pair of dumbbells.

Notice the characteristics for both barbells and dumbbells shown in Figure 14. On the

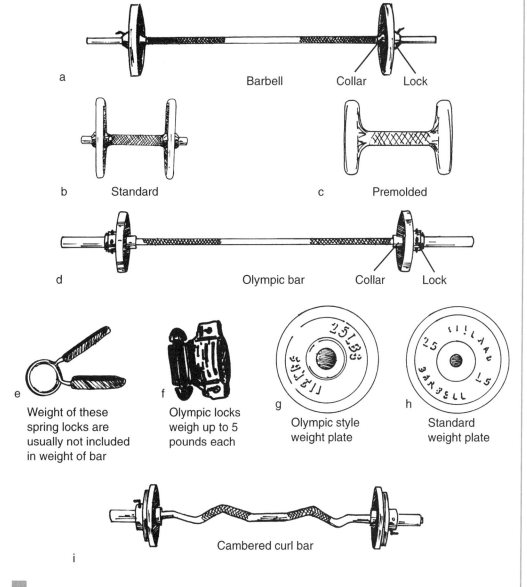

Figure 14 Free weight training equipment: typical barbell (a), standard and premolded dumbbells (b and c), Olympic bar (d), locks (e and f), Olympic-style weight plate (g), standard weight plate (h), and cambered bar (i).

typical barbell (Figure 14a), the middle section has both smooth and knurled, or roughened areas, and collars and locks on each end. The weight plates slide up to the collars, which stop the plates from sliding inward toward the hands. The outside locks (Figure 14e) slide up to the plates and keep them from sliding off the ends. A typical bar with collars and locks weighs approximately 5 pounds per foot; thus a 5-foot bar weighs approximately 25 pounds, and a 6-foot bar, 30 pounds. Dumbbells (Figures 14b and 14c) have a similar design except they are shorter and the entire middle section of the bar, between the weight plates, is usually knurled (roughened). The dumbbell bar with collars and locks weighs approximately 3 pounds but is not usually considered when the weight of the dumbbell is recorded. For example, a dumbbell with a 10-pound plate on each side is described as weighing 20 pounds, not 23 pounds.

The longest barbell in a weight room, an Olympic bar (Figure 14d), is 7 feet long and weighs 45 pounds without locks. The locks vary in shape (Figures 14e and 14f), and their individual weight may range from less than a pound to 5 pounds. Therefore, an Olympic bar with locks can weigh as much as 55 pounds. An Olympic bar has the same diameter as most bars in the weight room except for the section between the collar and the end of the bar, where the diameter is greater. This is an important distinction to recognize when loading the bar. Only the Olympic weight plates (Figure 14g), with larger diameter holes, will fit properly onto the Olympic bar. The plates with the smaller holes (Figure 14h) will not fit onto the Olympic bar.

Another type of bar is the cambered curl bar (Figure 14i). It has the same characteristics as the barbell, except that it has curves that enable you to isolate stress more effectively on certain muscle groups better than if a straight bar was being used.

Training Precautions With Free Weights

The use of free weight barbells and dumbbells requires higher levels of motor coordination than using machines. The freedom of movement allowed by free weights easily translates to potential injury when correct lifting, loading, and spotting techniques are not used. This is not to say that free weight training is dangerous. When reasonable precautions are taken, it is a very safe form of training and can be even more effective than machines in strengthening joint structures.

As you become more familiar with the free weight equipment, you will quickly realize that barbells and dumbbells offer tremendous versatility—your choice of exercises to perform is virtually unlimited. If you plan to train at home, this versatility and the lower cost of free weights will make them the preferred type of equipment.

However, there are certain precautions that you should take. The following actions will help you avoid potentially dangerous situations and make free weight training safer.

Load Bars Properly

Take great care to add the proper amount of weight and, when doing so, to load the ends of bars evenly. The stress imposed on muscles due to an unexpected overly loaded bar can easily cause injury. Also, if the ends of a bar (on the "flat" or incline bench and on the squat rack supports) are not loaded evenly, serious injury can occur to you and those nearby. Learning the weight of the weight plates and staying alert when loading each end of a bar will help a great deal to avoid these errors.

Lock Barbells and Dumbbells

Lifting with unlocked barbells and dumbbells is truly dangerous. Plates not secured with locks easily slide off the bar and can land on feet or other body parts. Locks should be checked for tightness before each set of exercises. Do not assume that the last person using the barbell or dumbbell tightened the locks. Also check to see that the collars are secure.

Avoid Backing Into Others

Because of sudden losses of balance or simply being unaware that anyone is near you, you may back into someone. Take care to avoid this, as an untimely bump may cause a barbell or dumbbell held overhead to be dropped on the head (from a standing press), a dumbbell to be dropped into the face (as in the supine dumbbell fly exercise), or any of a variety of other injuries.

Be Aware of Extended Bars

Extended bars are those that overhang or extend outward from machines, barbells supported on racks (e.g., on the squat rack) or uprights (as for the bench press), or bars held in the hands. Of special concern are bars positioned at or above shoulder height that you may bump into, causing serious facial injuries. Lat pull-down bars and free weight barbells held at or above shoulder height are the most likely sources of such injuries. Be especially cautious around people who are performing overhead exercises.

Store Equipment Properly

Each piece of equipment in a training facility should have a special storage location. Barbells, dumbbells, and weight plates left unattended, and those not replaced in their proper locations are often tripped over or slipped on. See that the equipment you use is always placed in appropriate racks and locations. This applies to your equipment at home as well as to the equipment in training facilities. There is an added danger if children have access to and are able to climb on equipment and lift plates and bars that are too heavy for them. Care should be taken to secure weight training equipment so that children do not have access to it without your supervision.

Using a Weightlifting Belt

A safety consideration not yet mentioned concerns that of using a weightlifting belt. It is common to see a weightlifting belt similar to that shown in Figure 15 being worn by men and women. Their use may contribute to injury-free training, but they will not in and of themselves protect you from back injuries—only good technique will. The appropriateness of their use is dependent on the exercise being performed and the relative amount of the load being used. You should wear a belt in those exercises that stress the back and involve maximum or near maximum loads. When using a belt, pull it snugly into position around the waist and be sure to breath properly during its use. Performing exercises with a belt too tight and/or not breathing properly can contribute to dizziness, blackouts, and cardiovascular complications.

Figure 15 Woman wearing weightlifting belt.

DRILLS

Becoming familiar with the various types of weight training equipment and how they are used safely is a logical starting point if you have not trained before. This involves being able to identify what the equipment is designed to do and how to use it, and determining whether it is in good working order. It is unwise to train on any piece of equipment until these things are known. Modify the following drills to best fit your situation to test your understanding of the concepts covered.

1. What Equipment Is Available?

Survey the equipment that is available in your facility. What different types do you recognize?

Success Goal = Place a check mark to the right of all the equipment that you observe.

Machine Equipment
    a. Fixed resistance___
    b. Variable resistance___
      Pivot ___
      Cam ___
    c. Isokinetic ___

Free Weight Equipment
    a. Standard bar ___
    b. Olympic bar ___
    c. Cambered curl bar ___
    d. Dumbbells ___

2. Equipment Safety Review

Safety is so important that you need to get in the habit of doing mental checks each time that you work out. Walk through the following checks with the equipment that you will use in your facility. Then, repeat this process each time that you work out.

Success Goal = Place a check mark to the left of each item as it is completed.

Machine Equipment Safety Checklist
    a. Before Each Training Session:
      ___ Check for frayed cables, belts, pulleys, worn chains, loose pads
      ___ Check for proper lever and seat adjustments
    b. During Training Sessions:
      ___ Assume a stable position on seats and pads
      ___ Fasten belts securely (if applicable)
      ___ Insert selector keys/pins properly
      ___ Perform exercises in a slow, controlled manner

Free Weight Equipment Safety Checklist
    a. Before Performing Each Set:

___ Check for integrity of collar welds
___ Check for tightness of collars and locks
___ Check for correct load on both ends of bar
b. During Each Training Session:
    ___ Avoid walking into bars that extend outward
    ___ Avoid walking near people performing overhead lifts
    ___ Avoid backing into others
    ___ Perform exercises in a slow, controlled manner
c. After Each Training Session:
    ___ Return equipment to its proper location

TRAINING FOR SUCCESS

As you begin your training, there are some suggestions that will make training more fun, safer, and more effective. The essentials to productive training that are outlined here are discussed in more detail later.

Train on a Regular Basis

The adage "Use it or lose it" is, unfortunately, true when it comes to maintaining cardiovascular efficiency, muscular strength and endurance, flexibility, and lean muscle mass. The body is unlike any machine yet to be developed. The body's efficiency improves with use, in contrast to machines, and it deteriorates with disuse. Sporadic training slows down the attainment of goals and has been the demise of many with good intentions. All too often, cessation of a regular training program begins with an innocent day of missing a workout and ends with missing many more. With each training session missed, the goal of improved fitness, strength, and appearance moves farther out of reach. It is important not to miss that first workout, because decreases in training status begin to occur after 72 hours of no training.

As researchers undertake studies involving older populations, it becomes apparent that individuals who follow regular exercise programs maintain their fitness levels, while those who do not can expect to lose as much as one pound of muscle per decade. Herbert deVries, a well-respected researcher, contends that much of the strength loss observed in older individuals is as much a function of sedentary living as it is an outcome of the aging process.

Gradually Increase Training Intensity

The body adapts to the stresses of weight training when training occurs on a regular basis, and when the intensity of training sessions is progressively increased over a reasonable period of time. Conversely, when the intensity of training is haphazard, the body's ability to adapt and become stronger and more enduring is seriously compromised. The dramatic improvements typically observed in response to training do not happen under these conditions, and the excitement that prompts you to continue training is no longer present. As excitement dwindles, attendance at training sessions becomes more and more difficult, and improvements become nonexistent. Muscle soreness does not go away, discouraging your enthusiasm for training even more.

Be Willing to Persevere

To maximize the time spent in training, you must learn to push yourself to the uncomfortable point of muscle failure during many of your sets. You must be willing to persevere through the discomfort (not pain) that accompanies reaching this point. Believing that weight training can make dramatic changes in your health and physique—which it definitely can—is essential to making the commitment to train hard and with regularity. Typically, you will feel the difference in muscle tone (firmness) immediately, and strength and endurance changes become somewhat noticeable after the second or third week. Be prepared, however, for variations in performance during the early stages of training, and do not become discouraged if one workout does not produce the outcomes of a previous one.

Your brain is going through a learning curve, too, as it tries to figure out which muscles to "recruit" (call into action) for which movement in each exercise. Thus, it is a time in which your neuromuscular system (your brain, nerves, and muscles) is learning to adapt to the stimulus of training. Be patient! This period is soon followed by significant gains in muscle tone and strength and decreased muscle soreness. This is truly an exciting time in your program! At this point your attitude dictates the magnitude of the future gains you will experience.

Strive for Quality Reps

Many people seem to believe that more repetitions in an exercise is synonymous with improvement, regardless of the technique used during execution. The speed with which they are performed is a very important factor in your ability to execute quality reps. In exercise programs designed to develop power, explosive exercise movements are required. However, in a beginning program, slow, controlled movements are desired. Consider "slow" to mean that approximately 2 seconds are used to complete the upward phase and 4 seconds for the downward phase of an exercise. It is especially important that exercises be performed at a rate slow enough to permit full extension and flexion at a joint (e.g., in the biceps curl, the elbow is fully extended and then fully flexed). Jerking, slinging, and using momentum are not recommended ways to complete a repetition. *Remember that the quality of the performed exercise should be viewed as being more important than simply the number of repetitions performed*, especially when the goal is improved flexibility. Other recommendations concerning proper exercise execution are provided in Steps 3 through 8.

Always Warm Up and Cool Down

Workouts should always begin with some warm-up exercises so that the muscles are better prepared to meet the challenges presented by various exercises. A cool-down period will help to provide the opportunity for your muscles to recover, and offer an excellent opportunity to work on flexibility. An example of appropriate warm-up and cool-down exercises to use are presented in Step 2.

Eat Smart

Nutrition is a key factor. It makes no sense to train hard if you are not also eating nutritionally sound meals. Poor nutrition in itself can reduce strength, muscular endurance, and muscle hypertrophy. Because training puts great demands on your body, your body needs nutrients to encourage adaptation and promote gains. To neglect this aspect of your training program is definitely an oversight if you are serious about improving. A more detailed discussion is provided in the section "Nutritional and Body Weight Issues."

Build in Days of Rest

The intervening days of rest in your training program are very important to gains in strength, muscular endurance, and size. To train on consecutive days without the rest that allows the body to recuperate may result in injury, a plateauing in gains, or a drop in performance. Properly timed rest is as important to your strength gains as training on a regular basis.

Obtain Medical Clearance

A history or presence of joint (e.g., arthritis, surgery), respiratory (e.g., asthma), or cardio-vascular (e.g., hypertension, arrhythmias, murmurs) problems, may or may not make weight training exercises an inappropriate activity to undertake; however, the implications of such conditions must be addressed before developing an exercise program, and certainly before exercise actually begins. Refer to Table 1 and carefully consider the questions presented. If you answer "yes" to any of them, consult a physician prior to beginning a training program.

Table 1   Medical Clearance Checklist
You should consult a physician before beginning a weight training program if you answer "yes" to any of the following questions.

Yes	No	
___	___	Have you had surgery or experienced bone, muscle, tendon, or ligament problems (especially back or knee) that might be aggravated by an exercise program?
___	___	Are you over age 50 (female) or 40 (male) and not accustomed to exercise?
___	___	Do you have a history of heart disease?
___	___	Has a doctor ever said your blood pressure was too high?
___	___	Are you taking any prescription medications, such as those for heart problems or high blood pressure?
___	___	Have you ever experienced chest pain, spells of severe dizziness, or fainting?
___	___	Do you have a history of respiratory problems such as asthma?
___	___	Is there a good physical or health reason not already mentioned why you should not follow a weight training program?

Note. From Fitness Weight Training (p. 24) by T.R. Baechle & R.W. Earle, 1995, Champaign, IL: Human Kinetics. Copyright 1995 by Human Kinetics Publishers.

STEP 1

LIFTING FUNDAMENTALS: MASTERING THE BASICS

Thus far you have gained a knowledge of the physiology behind weight training and of the equipment you will use. It is now an ideal time to learn about and master fundamental lifting skills. These will be used in every workout, and can even be applied to everyday physical tasks at home and work.

Why Are Lifting Fundamentals Important?

Correctly performing basic lifting skills avoids placing excessive stress on muscles, tendons, ligaments, bones, and joints, therefore decreasing the likelihood of injury. Using proper lifting fundamentals also produces quicker training results because muscles can be properly stressed and stimulated more effectively. Learning to breathe properly is an important part of developing good fundamental lifting skills as well. Proper breathing helps avoid getting dizzy or having blackouts, which can lead to life-threatening circumstances. The fundamentals learned in this step can be applied to all exercises and spotting procedures described in this text. While you are learning these basic lifting and spotting skills, always use a dowel stick, a very light bar, or a light load selection on machines.

Correct Lifting Techniques

The techniques of lifting involve focusing on four things: (a) acquiring a good grip, (b) having a stable position from which to lift, (c) keeping the object being lifted close to the body, and (d) using your legs, not your back, when lifting bars off the floor.

Gripping the Bar

There are two things to consider when establishing a grip: the type of grip used, and where and how far apart the hands are positioned on the bar. The grips that may be used to lift a bar off the floor are the overhand, or pronated, grip; the underhand, or supinated, grip; and the alternated grip. Note that your palms are face down, or away, in the overhand grip (Figure 1.1a), and the thumbs face each other. In the underhand grip (Figure 1.1b), your palms are facing upward, or toward you, while the thumbs face away from each other. The alternated grip (Figure 1.1c),

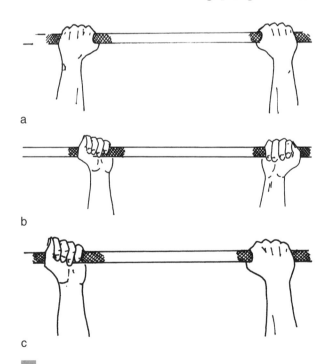

a

b

c

Figure 1.1 Closed bar grips: overhand (a), underhand (b), and alternated (c).

sometimes referred to as a mixed grip, involves having one hand in an underhand grip and the other in an overhand grip. In the alternated grip the thumbs point in the same direction. It does not matter which hand is positioned overhand or underhand in the alternated grip. All of these are termed closed grips, meaning that the fingers and thumbs are wrapped (closed) around the bar.

An open grip (Figure 1.2), sometimes referred to as a false grip, is one in which the thumbs do not wrap around the bar. The open grip is very dangerous because the bar can easily roll out of the hands onto the face or foot, causing severe injury. Always use a closed grip!

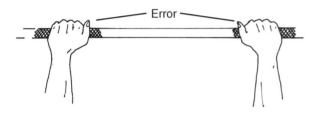

Figure 1.2 Improper grip: the open grip.

Width of Grip

Figure 1.3 shows several grip widths used in weight training. In some exercises the width of the grip places the hands at about shoulder width and equidistant from the weight plates. This is referred to as the "common" grip. Some exercises require a narrower grip, others a wider grip. Learn the proper width for each exercise, as well as where to place the hands so that the bar is held in a balanced position. Improperly gripped bars with weight plates that are not locked can result in weight plates falling or being catapulted off the ends of the bar, causing serious injury. Becoming familiar with the smooth and knurled areas of the bar, as discussed earlier, and where the hands should be placed on these areas will help you establish a balanced grip. Note that the grip used later in

explaining proper lifting techniques is the common grip.

Preparatory Lifting Position

Take hold of the bar using an overhand grip, and position the hands outside of the legs. Now move into the correct preparatory position shown in Figures 1.4 a and b. Shuffle your feet toward the bar so that your shins are almost touching it. Positioning the bar close to the shins keeps the weight being lifted closer to the body during the lifting/pulling action, enabling you to exert a more effective force with your legs (and avoiding straining your lower back). A key concept to remember is that a stable lifting position strategically positions the leg muscles to effectively contribute in lifting the barbell.

Establish a stable position by placing your feet flat on the floor, with the toes pointing slightly outward and the feet shoulderwidth apart or slightly wider. A wide stance or "base of support," provides greater stability and a more balanced lifting position. Establishing a stable position is especially important when performing overhead exercises with dumbbells or barbells. It is equally important when performing machine exercises that require the positioning of the feet on the floor, or the head, torso, hips, and legs on or against equipment.

Now imagine the position typically assumed by a gorilla. Believe it or not, this is the position that is ideal for lifting a barbell off the floor. Start by straightening your elbows as you lower your hips. Now position your shoulders over or slightly ahead of the bar while keeping the head up. Focus your eyes straight ahead. The back should be in a "flat" or slightly arched position. Establish a chest out and shoulders back position by pulling the scapulae (shoulder blades) toward each other. Avoid the rounded back position shown in Figure 1.4c.

Oftentimes one or both heels will lift up when moving into the low position shown in Figures 1.4 a and b, causing you to step forward in an effort to catch

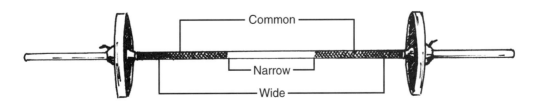

Figure 1.3 Grip widths: common, narrow, and wide.

your balance. If this happens, work on Drill 2 at the end of this step. Also realize that a proper head position (with the eyes looking straight ahead) is critical to maintaining proper body positioning. If there is a mirror available, watch yourself as you move into the low preparatory position. Does your back stay in a flat position, and do your heels stay in contact with the floor? Say these things to yourself: "Keep the bar close," "The hips stay low as the legs straighten," and "The back remains flat throughout the lifting." Keeping your head upright and your eyes looking straight ahead will help you accomplish these things. Get a mental picture of the head, shoulder, back, and hip positions shown. The most important things to remember are to keep the barbell, dumbbell, or weight plate as close as possible and to use your leg muscles, not your back! In preparation for pulling, breathe in to stabilize your upper torso.

<table>
<tr><td>FIGURE
1.4</td><td>**KEYS TO SUCCESS**</td></tr>
</table>

PREPARATORY LIFTING POSITION

Front View

1. Grip slightly wider than shoulder width ___
2. Feet shoulder-width apart ___
3. Feet flat on floor, toes pointed slightly outward ___
4. Hips low—"gorilla" position ___

a

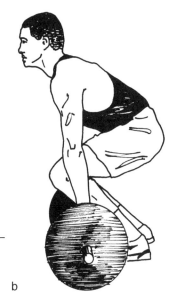

Side View

5. Arms straight, shoulders over or slightly forward of bar ___
6. Head up, eyes focused straight ahead (throughout exercise) ___
7. Back flat and tensed ___
8. Scapulae (shoulder blades) pulled toward each other ___
9. Chest held high ___

b

Error

c

Lifting the Bar

During the floor-to-thigh phase shown in Figures 1.5, a-c, pull the bar upward in a slow, controlled manner. Do not jerk the bar off the floor. Once the bar reaches the midthigh level, exhale. At this height the barbell or object may be placed in a rack or handed to a partner. Bringing the bar to this height may also be the first phase of a movement that takes the bar to a position at the shoulders in preparation for the overhead press exercise described in Step 5.

FIGURE 1.5 — **KEYS TO SUCCESS**

FLOOR-TO-THIGH PHASE

a   b   c

Position

1. Inhale before pulling ___
2. Slow, controlled pull ___
3. Back remains flat ___

Lift

4. Knees begin to straighten while hips stay low ___
5. Elbows remain straight ___
6. Bar remains close to shins, knees, and thighs ___

Straighten

7. Shoulders stay over the bar as knees straighten ___
8. Exhale when bar reaches midthigh ___

If you need to pull the barbell to your shoulders (thigh-to-shoulder execution phase, Figure 1.6, a-c), continue pulling; do not allow the bar to rest on your thighs and do not exhale yet. Instead, "brush" the bar against your thighs as you continue to pull upward. As you straighten your legs, your hips move forward quickly. Follow this with a rapid shoulder shrug using the trapezius muscles (between the neck and shoulder). Exhale immediately after the shrug. Typically you will raise up on the balls of your feet at this point, as shown in Figure 1.6b. Visualize yourself jumping with the barbell while keeping your elbows straight. At the very peak of the shrug (and the bar's acceleration), your elbows flex and the bar is racked (caught) on the shoulders. Finish the racking movement by moving your elbows upward and forward (Figure 1.6c). During the pulling action, keep the bar close and your elbows straight until your legs straighten completely (see front view in Figure 1.6d). Keep your elbows pointed outward and your wrists below the elbows (Figure 1.6d) for as long as possible during the pull (i.e., before flexing them in the catching or racking movement). Time the racking of the bar onto your shoulders so that your knees and hips are flexed as the bar makes contact. This will help to absorb the force of the bar's impact on your shoulders. Breathe out immediately after you have reached the highest point of the shrug.

FIGURE 1.6 **KEYS TO SUCCESS**

THIGH-TO-SHOULDER PHASE

a

Jump

1. Bar "brushes" middle or top of thighs ___
2. Bar kept close to body as hips drive forward ___
3. Elbows remain straight until legs and hips straighten completely ___

b

Shrug

4. Shrug quickly to accelerate bar ___
5. Shrug as high as possible before flexing elbows ___

c

Catch

6. As elbows flex, pull them upward and keep them above the wrists ___
7. Elbows rotate around bar ___
8. Bar is caught (racked) on the shoulders, knees flex to absorb bar ___
9. Upright stance, elbows up, chest high ___

Front View

a. Pulling action occurs between Figures a and b ___
b. Elbows are upward, not pulled back ___

d

Returning the Bar to the Floor

When lowering the bar or any other heavy object to the floor, use what you have learned about establishing a stable position, keeping the bar close and the back flat, and using your legs instead of your back to lower the bar. Also remember to lower the bar to the floor in a slow, controlled manner.

With the bar at shoulder height as shown (Figure 1.7a), allow its weight to slowly pull your arms to a straightened position (Figure 1.7b), which should very briefly place the bar in a resting position on your thighs. Your hips and knees should be flexed so that, as the bar touches your thigh, its weight is absorbed momentarily before it is lowered to the floor. Remem-

ber to keep your head up and back flat throughout the bar's return to the floor (Figure 1.7c)

Breathing

The best time to exhale in most exercises is during the "sticking point," or the most difficult point in a repetition. Inhalation should occur during the relaxation phase, or easiest point in a repetition. For example, in the upward movement of the biceps curl, exhalation should occur when the forearm reaches perpendicular with the floor, the most difficult point in the repetition. Inhalation should occur as the bar

FIGURE 1.7 | **KEYS TO SUCCESS**

SHOULDER-TO-FLOOR PHASE

a   b   c

Lower   **Pause**   **Return**

1. Bar is lowered to thighs first ___
2. Hips and knees flex to absorb weight ___

3. Back remains flat or slightly arched ___
4. Shoulders stay back ___
5. Bar stays close to thighs, knees, shins ___

6. Bar lowered under control to floor ___

is being lowered (the easiest point in the repetition). In exercises where upper torso stabilization is needed to help maintain a correct lifting position, such as in the squat or power clean (more advanced) exercises in Appendix A, breathing should occur at the very end of the sticking point. For exercises shown in Steps 2-8 and Appendix A, remember to breathe out through the sticking point!

Be aware that you will have a tendency in most exercises to hold your breath too long. This should be avoided because it is dangerous! By not exhaling, you reduce the return of blood to your heart, which in turn reduces the blood flow to the brain. If the brain is deprived of oxygen-rich blood, you will become dizzy and may faint. Holding the breath too long is especially dangerous if you are performing overhead free weight exercises. If you have high blood pressure it is imperative that you: (1) consult a physician before you begin a weight training program; and (2) exhale through the sticking point in each repetition. Learning to exhale at the correct time can be confusing, but not in this text because you are told and shown when to exhale in each exercise.

Spotter's Responsibilities

A spotter assists and protects the person lifting from injury. Spotters play a crucial role in making weight training a safe activity. If you are asked to be a spotter, realize that being inattentive can cause very serious injury (muscle/tendon tears, facial and other bone fractures, broken teeth, etc.). Not all exercises require spotters, but exercises such as the free weight bench press, back squat, and those involving overhead pressing movements must be spotted. Just as you may need to rely on spotters, the individuals you spot are relying on you. Do not underestimate the significance of your responsibilities as a spotter. Read and adhere to the following guidelines for spotting free weight exercises and for being responsible to the spotter when you are lifting. Specific instructions for spotting are provided later in this text for the exercises in which a spotter is recommended.

Guidelines for Spotting Free Weight Exercises

Remember: Spotters with poor technique can be injured, too!

1. Remove all loose plates, barbells, and dumbbells from the area to avoid slipping or tripping on them.
2. Learn and practice the Keys to Success Spotting Techniques/Procedures when they are presented.
3. Place your body in a good lifting position in case you have to "catch" the bar (keep your knees flexed and your back flat).
4. Effectively communicate with the person you are spotting (e.g., know how many reps they intend to complete).
5. Use the appropriate grip (a closed grip is a must!) with the proper hand location on the bar (if you need to grip the bar).
6. See that the bar is properly and evenly loaded.
7. Be knowledgeable about dangerous and potentially dangerous situations associated with the exercise being performed. (These will be identified throughout the text.)
8. Be alert and quick to respond to dangerous situations.
9. Know when and how to guide the bar in the desired path.
10. Know when and how much lifting assistance is needed to complete the exercise.
11. As a last resort, assume all of the weight of the bar, but only if the person you are spotting might be injured if you don't.
12. Suggest appropriate form changes as necessary.

Your Responsibilities (as the One Lifting) to the Spotter

As the person lifting, your actions are important to the safety of your spotter as well as yourself. Following these suggestions will help make training safer for both of you.

1. Communicate the number of reps you intend to complete before the exercise begins.
2. Indicate when you need assistance.
3. Always stay with the bar. That is, once the spotter needs to assist, remember not to release the bar or stop trying to complete the exercise. If you do, the spotter must assume the entire weight of the bar and might be injured.
4. Learn your limits, and select appropriate loads and reps. (This is a common problem for individuals new to training.)

LIFTING FUNDAMENTALS SUCCESS STOPPERS

Approach the detection of errors with the thought that recognizing errors will enable you to quickly develop excellent lifting skills. The errors that follow are typical. Of special concern are (a) the knees straightening immediately during the floor-to-thigh phase, (b) the elbows flexing too soon during the thigh-to-shoulder phase, and (c) not lowering the hips in the shoulder-to-floor phase.

Error	Correction
Floor-to-Thigh Phase	
1. Your heels raise up.	1. Too much weight is on the balls of your feet. You may be leaning too far forward. "Sit back" into the low position, and concentrate on putting more weight on your heels.
2. Your upward pull is not smooth.	2. Straighten your elbows before pulling, and pull slowly.
3. Your hips raise up first when pulling.	3. This puts stress on your back rather than your legs. Your knees are straightening too soon! Think, "My upward movement is led with my shoulders, not my hips." This will enable you to use your legs instead of your back to do the lifting.
Thigh-to-Shoulder Phase	
1. Bar stops on your thighs.	1. The pull from the floor to your thighs should be continuous. Do not allow yourself to pause or stop the bar at your thighs.
2. Bar swings away from your thighs and hips.	2. Concentrate on pulling the bar up straight and keeping it in close to your thighs and hips.
3. Your elbows flex too soon.	3. Wait until your shrug is at its highest point before flexing your elbows.
4. Your knees are straight when racking.	4. Having your knees flexed provides "give" to your shoulders as you rack the bar on them, dissipating much of the impact.
Shoulder-to-Floor Phase	
1. Bar does not pause at your thighs.	1. Visualize the downward phase as a 2-count movement, "1" to the thigh, "2" to the floor.
2. Your hips remain high while lowering the bar from thigh height to the floor.	2. This is stressful on the back! Once the bar reaches the thighs, squat down to lower the bar while keeping an upright and flat-back position.

LIFTING FUNDAMENTALS DRILLS

1. Grip Selection and Location

This drill involves lifting an empty bar or a dowel stick from the floor using the three types of grips in the three grip-width positions described earlier. When completing this drill the hands should be positioned on the bar so that it is balanced when being pulled to the thighs. Now using an overhand grip (Figure 1.1a), lift the bar to the thighs and then lower it back to the floor using correct lifting techniques. Lift the bar twice more to your thighs, using first the underhand grip (Figure 1.1b) and then the alternated grip (Figure 1.1c). Now move your hands to the common grip width and use the three different types of grips. Next move your hands to the narrow grip and do the same. Perform all grips with your thumbs around the bar. Check off each type of grip in which the grip and grip widths are performed correctly.

Success Goal = 9 total reps using 3 grip widths in each grip
- a. 3 overhand grip reps ___
- b. 3 underhand grip reps ___
- c. 3 alternated grip reps ___

Success Check
- Establish the proper hand spacing ___
- Keep the thumbs around bar ___
- Remember the names of the grips ___

2. Preparation Position

This drill will help you develop a better sense of balance and a greater awareness of proper body positioning. Without falling forward or rising up on either or both heels, squat down into the "gorilla" position with your hands clasped behind your head. Performing this drill in front of a mirror is a great way to critique and perfect your technique. Move into the gorilla position 10 times.

Success Goal = 10 reps performed with good balance ___

Success Check
- Heels on floor, back flat ___
- Head upright ___
- Eyes straight ahead ___

3. Floor-to-Thigh Drill

This drill is designed to assist you in learning to keep the bar in close to your shins, knees, and thighs, avoiding lower back injury when lifting and returning the bar to the floor. From a standing position, move into the preparatory ("gorilla") lifting position and, using the overhand grip, pull the bar to the middle of your thighs. Remember good lifting techniques: head up, back flat, and let the legs do the lifting. Lower the bar to the floor in the same manner. Repeat this drill 10 times.

Success Goal = 10 total reps performed with good lifting technique ___

Success Check
- Maintain flat back with head up ___
- Feel the shoulders-back position ___
- Keep hips low ___

4. Shrug Drill

Most beginners have a great tendency to flex the elbows too soon during what is commonly referred to as the second pull—that is, the pull at the thigh that brings the bar to the shoulders. This drill will help you avoid this common technique flaw. Using an overhand grip, pick up the bar and hold it at midthigh. With your knees and hips slightly flexed, perform a quick shoulder shrug, followed immediately by hip and knee extension while keeping your elbows straight. You may want to think of the movement as jumping with a bar while keeping your elbows straight. After each jump, return the bar to your thighs (not to the floor). Repeat this drill 10 times.

Success Goal = 10 jumps (reps) with straight elbows ___

Success Check
- Feel the stretch in the "traps" ___

5. Racking the Bar Drill

This drill will help you develop the timing you need to flex your hips and knees when racking the bar on your shoulders. Follow the same procedures used in the previous drill, but instead of lowering the bar after the jump, pull the bar to your shoulders. Work on timing the "catch" of the bar at your shoulders with the flexing of your hips and knees and with your feet moving to a stance that is somewhat wider than in the initial position.

Success Goal = 10 reps are racked with the hips, knees, and feet properly positioned ___

Success Check
- Cushion the catch on the shoulders by flexing the knees ___
- Remember, elbows straight until hips are fully extended ___

LIFTING FUNDAMENTALS SUCCESS SUMMARY

Good lifting technique requires a proper grip, a stable position from which to lift, keeping the object being lifted close to your body, and using your legs rather than your back. Remember, "Hips stay low as the legs straighten." This is true regardless of whether you are lifting a barbell (review Figures 1.5-1.7), lifting a box off the floor, or spotting in an exercise. Developing good fundamental techniques will help you avoid injury and work muscles in ways that produce optimal results.

STEP 2

PRACTICE PROCEDURES: LEARNING THE PROCESS

A cquiring the ability to perform weight training exercises correctly creates a sense of accomplishment and pride, and enables you to make each training session more satisfying and productive. You will be able to apply the basic lifting techniques you just mastered in Step 1 as you are guided through practice procedures for learning the exercises in Steps 3-8.

Why Is Learning the Practice Procedures Important?

"Practice makes perfect" is the underlying theme for the manner in which this step has been developed and organized. It consists of procedures that have been logically organized into a series of five practice activities, called practice procedures. Insight gained from these practice procedures will help you to learn exercises quickly and in a safe manner, and in the process increase your confidence, enjoyment, and weight training success. These procedures are as follows:

1. Choose one exercise.
2. Determine trial and warm-up loads.
3. Practice proper technique.
4. Determine training load.
5. Make needed load adjustments.

Detailed descriptions of each of these practice procedures follow.

1. Choose One Exercise

Within Steps 3 through 8, you will be given a variety of choices to help you start your weight training program. First, you will be choosing one exercise for each

of the seven muscle groups shown in Figure 2.1 a and b, and then recording the name of your exercise selection in the "Exercise" column on the workout chart in Appendix C. Each step usually includes a choice of one free weight and two machine exercises. Read the exercise technique explanations for each and view the Keys to Success. Consider the equipment and spotting requirements of each exercise. After Step 8, make at least three copies of the workout chart in Appendix C.

2. Determine Trial and Warm-Up Loads

Using light loads in the early stages of learning weight training exercises enables you to concentrate more on the techniques required of the exercise and less on how hard to push or pull. Out of enthusiasm or curiosity, you may be tempted to use loads that are too heavy. Selecting loads that are too heavy, even if your technique is perfect, increases the chances of injury. Avoid this temptation!

This practice procedure explains how to use the formulas shown in Figure 2.2 to determine the warm-up and trial loads for most exercises. Once you have your exercise selection, you will need to identify the coefficient associated with that exercise in Figure 2.2. The letters FW (for free weight), C (for cam), and M (for multi-unit—can be single-unit too) are used to assist you in doing this. Realize that the coefficients are estimates. The unique differences of individuals combined with the variance in equipment design make it difficult, if not impossible, to derive coefficients that are without error. Those presented in this text are starting points for determining appropriate loads.

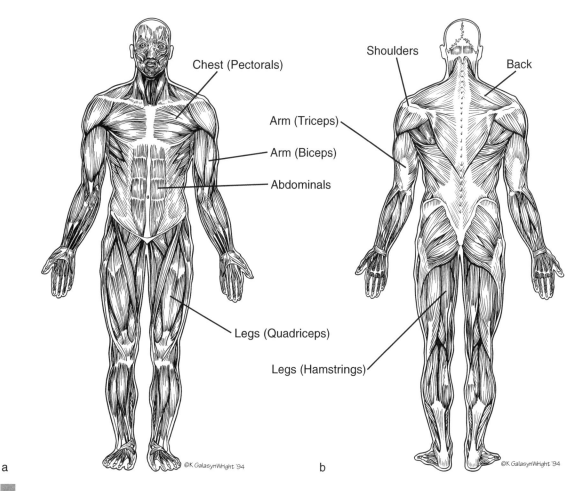

Chest (Pectorals)

Arm (Triceps)

Arm (Biceps)

Abdominals

Legs (Quadriceps)

Legs (Hamstrings)

Shoulders

Back

©K. GalasynWright '94

a

b

©K. GalasynWright '94

Figure 2.1 Muscle groups: anterior (front, a) and posterior (back, b) views. Exercises for each of these muscle groups are included in the basic program. © K. Galasyn-Wright, Champaign, IL, 1994.

After you've located the name of the exercise selected, fill in your body weight in the appropriate space and multiply it by the number to the right of it (the coefficient). The use of body weight in determining appropriate loads is based upon the relationship that body weight has to strength. This is the same logic used for creating weight divisions in such sports as wrestling, boxing, and weightlifting. The coefficient is a number that has been derived from studies of males and females experienced and inexperienced in weight training. When multiplied by your body weight, the coefficient can be used in estimating training loads; using one-half of it provides an appropriate warm-up load. Note that if you are a male who weighs more than 175 pounds simply record your body weight as 175. If you are a female and weigh over 140 pounds record your body weight as 140.

Using this method sometimes results in a warm-up load for women that is lighter than the lightest weight-stack plate on a machine. If this occurs, se-lect the lightest weight plate and recruit someone who is experienced to safely assist (by pushing or pulling) in accomplishing the movement patterns involved in the exercise. The bars available for free weight exercises may pose the same problems. If so, very light dumbbells, a stripped-down dumbbell bar, or a single weight plate may be used during warm-up sets. A wooden dowel stick (less than a pound in weight) can even be used.

To complete this procedure, round off numbers to the nearest 5-pound increment or to the closest weight-stack plate. This becomes your trial load. The example in Figure 2.2 is of a female who weighs 120 pounds and has selected the free weight bench press from the three chest exercises available. In this example the rounded-off trial load equals 40 pounds, and one-half equals a warm-up load of 20 pounds (bottom section of Figure 2.2). The warm-up load is used in learning the exercise techniques in practice procedure 3, while the trial load is used in practice

Trial Load Determination Formula CHEST					
Body weight	(Exercise)	×	Coefficient	=	Trial load
Female					
BWT= *120*	(FW-bench press)	×	.35	=	*42 rounded off = 40 pounds ÷ 2 = 20 pounds (warm-up load)*
BWT= ____	(C-bent-arm fly)	×	.14	=	____
BWT= ____	(M-chest press)	×	.27	=	____
Male					
BWT= ____	(FW-bench press)	×	.60	=	____
BWT= ____	(C-bent-arm fly)	×	.30	=	____
BWT= ____	(M-chest press)	×	.55	=	____

BWT= body weight, FW = free weight, C = cam, and M = multi- or single-unit machine exercise.
Note. If you are a male who weighs more than 175 pounds (79.25 kg), then record your body weight as 175 (79.25 kg). If you are a female and weigh over 140 pounds (63.5 kg), then record your body weight as 140 (63.5 kg).

Figure 2.2 Calculating warm-up and trial loads.

procedure 4 to determine the training load. Note that the term *trial load* is used because you will be "trying it out" in practice procedure 4 to see if it is an appropriate load to use later for training. Trial loads that are too heavy or light can be adjusted using practice procedure 5.

3. Practice Proper Technique

In this practice procedure you will use warm-up loads while learning each exercise's

- grip,
- body positioning,
- movement pattern,
- bar velocity, and
- breathing pattern.

Carefully read the information and directions provided next concerning each of these technique considerations and make a concerted effort to apply them during practice procedure 3 in Steps 3-8.

Grip

As you have learned in Step 1, there are a variety of weight training grips (and grip widths) that can be used. Learn which is the appropriate type of grip to use and where to place the hands when using that grip in each exercise.

Body Positioning

Body positioning refers to the initial posture of the body, not arm or leg movements. Proper positioning in lying or standing exercises, or on equipment, provides a balanced and stable position from which to pull or push. Improper positioning can reduce the benefits of an exercise or result in serious injury.

Movement Pattern

The movement pattern refers to how the arms, legs, and trunk move during the execution of an exercise, and includes consideration of the need to complete the full range of movement. Performing exercises through the movement ranges and in the patterns shown in this text enables you to get the arms, legs, and trunk more active during each rep and, therefore, better trained. Learning and practicing the correct movement patterns and ranges also contribute to safer training sessions.

Bar Velocity

Velocity refers to the speed of movement as the barbell/dumbbell/handle moves through the range of motion in an exercise. It is especially important during this practice procedure that you establish the habit of performing slow, controlled movement patterns. Try to allow about 2 seconds for the concentric (usually upward movement) and 4 seconds for the eccentric (downward) phases of the exercise. Doing so will avoid the buildup of momentum that is commonly associated with weight training injuries.

Breathing Pattern

Trying to remember when to exhale and inhale can be confusing, especially when there are other skills to remember at the same time. As you practice performing exercises with warm-up loads, learn to identify where in each exercise the "sticking point" occurs and breathe out as described in Step 1. Remember that the sticking point is that phase in a repetition where it becomes most difficult. Inhale during the recovery movement phase.

4. Determine Training Load

This procedure is designed to help you determine an appropriate training load, one that will result in muscular failure on the 12th to 15th rep when giving a maximum effort. Simply use the trial load determined in practice procedure 2, and perform as many reps as possible. If the number of reps completed is 12 to 15, you have found an appropriate training load to use. Record this load on the workout chart in Appendix C under the "Training load" column. If you performed less than 12 or more than 15 reps in any of Steps 3 through 8, you have one more practice procedure to complete before moving on to the next exercise and establishing its training load.

5. Make Needed Load Adjustments

Because individuals differ in physical characteristics and experience, and because weight training equipment differs in design, trial loads may not produce the desired range of 12 to 15 reps. If you performed less than 12 reps with the trial load, it is too heavy. On the other hand, if you performed more than 15 reps, the load is too light. In this practice procedure you will use your trial loads and a load adjustment chart to make necessary adjustments. Once training begins you may need to use the adjustment chart several times before an accurate training load is determined. Figure 2.3 a and b, shows how the Load Adjustment Chart and the formula for determining the Training Load are used to make needed adjustments to your trial load. The example given is of someone who performed 9 reps with 100 pounds in the free weight bench press exercise. Because only 9 reps (instead of 12-15 reps) were performed (too heavy), there is a need to reduce the load.

As you can see in Figure 2.3, 9 reps are associated with a 10-pound reduction that results in a training load of 90 pounds. When needed, this procedure adjusts the trial load to create an appropriate training load for you.

Follow these same procedures for recording all exercises and training loads. Be sure to record the exercise you selected for the chest first (at the top) on

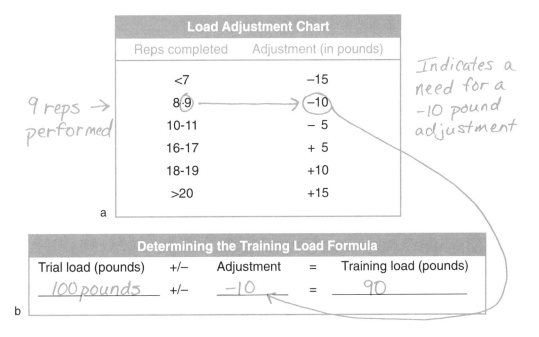

Figure 2.3 Making load adjustments. Load adjustment chart (a). Determining the training load formula (b).

1. Choose One Exercise

After reading about the characteristics and techniques involved in the three different exercises and the type of equipment required for each, you are ready to put what you have learned to use. Consider the availability of equipment and access to spotters in your situation, then select one of the following exercises to use in your program:

- Free weight bench press
- Bent-arm fly (cam machine)
- Chest press (multi- or single-unit weight machine)

Turn to Appendix C and copy your chest exercise choice onto the workout chart in the "Exercise" column.

Success Goal = 1 chest exercise selected and recorded ✓

Success Check
- Consider availability of equipment ___
- Consider need for spotter ___
- Consider time available ___

Your choice = _Bench press_

Determining the Training Load Formula

Trial load (pounds)	+/−	Adjustment	=	Training load (pounds)
100	+/−	−10	=	90

Weight Training Workout Chart (3-Days-a-W...

Name _Tom Brown_

Week # _____

Order	Muscle area	Exercise	Training load	Set	Day 1			Day 2			D
					1	2	3	1	2	3	1
1	Chest	Bench press	90	Wt.							
				Reps							
2	Back	Bent over row	80	Wt.							
				Reps							
3	Shoulder	Standing press	60	Wt.							
				Reps							
4	Arms (front of)	Bicep curl	75	Wt.							
				Reps							
5	Arms (back of)	Tricep press down	30	Wt.							
				Reps							
6	Legs	Leg press	165	Wt.							
				Reps							
7	Abdomen	Twisting trunk curl	—	Wt.							
				Reps							

Figure 2.4 Recording exercise selection and training load information.

the workout chart, then (below it) the exercises selected for the back, shoulders, arms (front, biceps—back, triceps), legs, and abdomen, in that order, as shown in Figure 2.4.

Visualization is an excellent method to help establish in your mind correct exercise and spotting techniques. Even though this is *not* a practice procedure listed in Steps 3-8, make an effort just before procedures 3 and 4 to use this technique. In it you use all of your senses while visualizing the correct execution of an exercise. Try to find a quiet location in the weight room, or develop the ability, even under noisy conditions, to clearly visualize the proper grip, body positioning, movement pattern, barbell/dumbbell/bar/handle velocity, and breathing for each exercise. Concentrate on feedback from your muscles and joints as you mentally rehearse exercises. This will help in learning how it "feels" when you are performing the exercise correctly. You may also want to mimic the correct movement patterns of exercises in front of a mirror, making note of the feedback you are sensing from muscles, tendons, and joints. Attempt to do this for 1 to 2 minutes immediately before you begin each exercise in practice procedure 3. As the opportunity arises, try to find time before each training session to visualize the proper techniques of each exercise until each has been mastered.

Warm Up and Cool Down

Because of the demands placed on the muscles and joints, it is important to warm up properly before each training session. Warm-up activities such as brisk walking or jogging in place for about 5 minutes, followed by an appropriate stretching routine, help to physically and mentally prepare you to train. The stretching will also improve your flexibility, or your ability to move joints through a full range of motion, and in doing so may help prevent injury. Go through a warm-up activity and then follow the series of static (held) stretching positions described and illustrated here. Be sure to move slowly into the stretched positions—no bouncing. The stretches presented involve major joints and muscle groups, especially the less flexible muscles of the back of the legs, the upper and lower back, and the neck.

Include these stretching exercises prior to weight training and immediately after each training session. Brisk walking or jogging plus stretching increases blood and muscle temperatures, enabling muscles to contract and relax with greater ease. Stretching afterward helps speed your recovery from muscle

soreness. Most important, a proper warm-up helps to prevent injuries during training. Hold each of the stretching positions for 6 to 10 seconds, and repeat them two or three times if you wish to.

Chest and Shoulders

Grasp your hands together behind your back and slowly lift them upward (see Figure 2.5), or simply reach back as far as possible if you are not able to grasp your hands. For an additional stretch, bend at the waist and raise your arms higher.

Figure 2.5 Chest and shoulder stretch.

Upper Back, Shoulder, and Arm

With your right hand, grasp your left elbow and pull it slowly across your chest toward your right shoulder. You will feel tension along the outside of your left shoulder and arm (see Figure 2.6). Repeat with the other arm. You can vary this stretch by pulling across and down over your chest and upper stomach.

Shoulder and Triceps (Back of Upper Arm)

Bring both arms overhead and hold your left elbow with your right hand. Allow your left arm to bend at

Figure 2.6 Upper back, shoulder, and arm stretch.

the elbow, and let your left hand rest against the back of your right shoulder. Pull with your right hand to slowly move the left elbow behind your head until you feel a stretch (see Figure 2.7). Repeat with the other arm.

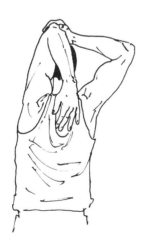

Figure 2.7 Shoulder and triceps stretch.

Back and Hip

Sit with your right leg straight. Bend your left leg, and cross your left foot over your right leg so it rests along the outside of your right knee with the sole flat on the floor. Then push against the outside of your upper left thigh, just above the knee, with your right elbow. Use your right elbow to keep this leg stationary as you perform the stretch. Next, place your left hand behind your buttocks, slowly turn your head to look over your left shoulder, and rotate your upper body toward your left hand and arm. You should feel tension in your lower back, hips, and buttocks (see Figure 2.8). Repeat with the other leg.

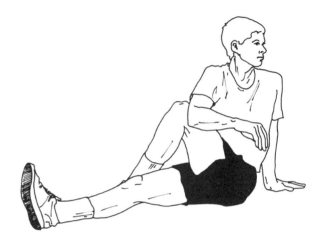

Figure 2.8 Back and hip stretch.

Back, Hamstring, and Inside-of-Thigh

While seated on the floor, straighten your right leg, with the sole of your left foot slightly touching the inside of your right knee. Bend from the hips slowly and slide the palms of the hands on the thighs toward your right ankle until you feel tension in the back of your right thigh (see Figure 2.9). Perform the same stretch with the left leg. Be sure to keep the

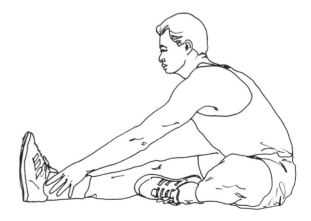

Figure 2.9 Back, hamstring, and inside-of-thigh stretch.

toes of your right foot pointing up while your ankles and toes are relaxed.

Quadriceps

This stretch is performed in the standing position. Use a wall or stationary object for balance, and grasp your right foot with the left hand and pull so that your heel moves back toward your buttocks. You should feel tension along the front of your right thigh (see Figure 2.10). Repeat with your left leg and right hand.

Calves

Stand facing a wall or stationary object about 2 feet away. With your feet together and your knees straight, lean forward. Apply a stretch on your calves by slowly moving your hips toward the wall. Be sure to keep your heels on the floor and your back straight (see Figure 2.11). You can stretch another muscle area of the calf by allowing the knees to flex slightly while in this same position.

Figure 2.10 Quadriceps stretch.

Figure 2.11 Calf stretch.

PRACTICE PROCEDURES

DRILLS

1. Self-Assessment Practice Procedure Quiz

Answer the following questions by checking off the correct answer:

1. The number of exercises you should choose in each of Steps 3 through 8 is [___ one, ___ two, ___ three].
2. In which practice procedure is the trial load used to determine your training load? [___ 2, ___ 3, ___ 4]
3. The warm-up load represents what percent of the trial load? [___ 25%, ___ 50%, ___ 75%]
4. If you performed 12 to 15 reps with the trial load, should you continue on to practice procedure 5? [___ yes, ___ no]

5. If you performed 17 reps with 100 pounds in practice procedure 4, what should your training load be? [___ 105 pounds, ___ 115 pounds, ___ 120 pounds]
6. By making needed adjustments to the trial load, you arrive at the [___ adjusted load, ___ training load].

Success Goal = Correctly answer all 6 questions ___

Self-Assessment Quiz Answers
1. one
2. 4
3. 50%
4. no
5. 105 pounds
6. training load

2. Warm-Up and Cool-Down Review

Before performing any of the exercises in Step 3 through 8, take time to review and practice the warm-up and cool-down exercises described in this step. Start with a brisk walk or jog in place for 5 minutes, then do an appropriate stretching exercises for the major joints and muscle groups, including the following: chest and shoulders; upper back, shoulder, and arm; shoulder and triceps; back and hip; back, hamstring, and inside-of-thigh areas; quadriceps (front-of-thigh area); and calves.

Hold each stretch for 6 to 10 seconds, and repeat two to three times. Avoid bouncing! Once you start training, remember to repeat two to three sets of each of these stretches after your workout as well.

Success Goal = 5 minutes of brisk walking or jogging, then 2 to 3 sets of at least 6 different stretches for the major muscle groups ___

Success Check
• Always warm-up before stretching ___
• Move slowly into the stretches ___
• Use static (versus ballistic) stretches ___

PRACTICE PROCEDURES SUCCESS SUMMARY

The procedures presented in this step are used in learning the exercises in Steps 3-8. You begin by selecting one of the three exercises shown in each of these steps. Next you determine and then use warm-up and trial loads with the Keys to Success to learn the exercise selected. If the loads are too heavy or too light, follow the adjustment guidelines given. Using the procedures in the order presented will make learning weight training exercises you select for your program very easy, especially if you practice visualizing the correct exercise techniques before procedures 3 and 4. Before performing any of the exercises in Steps 3-8, take time to review and practice the warm-up and cool-down exercises. Practicing them will serve as a warm-up and will provide an opportunity for you to learn how to perform them correctly. Be sure to start and end each training session with the warm-up/cool-down exercises.

STEP 3

CHEST EXERCISES: SELECTING ONE FOR YOUR PROGRAM

Some of the most popular exercises in weight training are those that work the chest muscles, or pectorals (pectoralis major, pectoralis minor), shown in the anterior view of Appendix B. When developed properly, these muscles contribute a great deal to an attractive upper body and to added success in many recreational athletic activities. The bench press, bent-arm fly, and chest press exercises described here provide an added benefit because they also work muscles of the shoulder (anterior deltoid). The bench press and chest press also work the back of the upper arm (triceps). Furthermore, the techniques involved are easily learned, and gains in muscular endurance and strength are made quickly.

Free Weight Exercise

If you have access to free weights, you may select the bench press exercise to develop your chest. If you prefer working with machines, see the "Machine Exercises" section.

How to Perform the Free Weight Bench Press

This exercise involves the use of a barbell and a bench with uprights (called a bench press bench). Begin by sitting on the far end of the bench with your back to the upright supports. Now lie back and position yourself so that your buttocks, shoulders, and head are firmly and squarely on the bench, as shown in Figure 3.1a. Your legs should straddle the bench, and your feet should be flat on the floor, about shoulder-width apart. This four-point position is important—

especially the straddled feet position—because it provides a stable position when handling the bar over your chest and face.

From this position, slide toward the upright supports until your eyes are directly below the front edge of the shelf (of the uprights). This position helps prevent the bar from hitting the uprights during the upward execution phase, yet keeps the bar close enough to be easily placed back onto the shelf ("racked") after the last repetition.

While the bar is supported on the uprights, grasp it with an evenly spaced overhand grip, hands about shoulder-width apart or wider. An appropriate grip width on the bar positions the forearms perpendicular to the floor as the bar touches the chest. Keep in mind that a wide grip emphasizes a larger area of the chest than a narrow one and is usually the preferred grip width.

From this position, push the bar off the uprights to a straight-elbow position with your wrists directly over your elbows. Pause with the bar in the extended-arm position, and then lower the bar slowly to your chest as shown in Figure 3.1b. The bar should contact your chest approximately an inch above or below the nipples. Inhale as you lower the bar to the chest. Once the bar touches the chest (do not bounce the bar off your chest), slowly push it straight upward to an extended-elbow position (see Figure 3.1c). Exhale through the sticking point, which occurs when the bar is about halfway up.

Throughout the exercise keep your head, shoulders, and buttocks in contact with the bench, and both feet flat on the floor. At the completion of the last repetition, signal it by saying "Okay." Then rack the bar. Be sure to support the bar until it is racked (see Figure 3.1d).

Spotting/Assistance Technique

As the spotter, you should stand forward of your partner's head about 2 to 6 inches from the bench and centered between the uprights (see Figure 3.1a). To assist your partner in moving the bar off the supports (termed "handing off"), grip the bar using the alternated grip. Space your hands evenly between your partner's hands. At his or her command, "Okay," carefully slide the bar off the supports and guide it to a straight-elbow position over the chest. Before releasing the bar, be sure that your partner's elbows are completely straight. Practice making your handoff as smooth as possible. If your handoff is too high or too low, or too far forward or too close to the shelf, it will disturb your partner's stable position on the bench, which may contribute to a poor performance or injury.

Once the downward phase begins, your hands and eyes follow the bar's path to the chest (see Figure 3.1b) and should lead the bar's upward movement (see Figure 3.1c). As the elbows straighten during the last repetition and after your partner has given the "okay" signal, assist by grasping the bar (see Figure 3.1d). Be sure that the bar is resting on the shelf of the upright supports before releasing it.

FIGURE 3.1 | **KEYS TO SUCCESS**

FREE WEIGHT BENCH PRESS

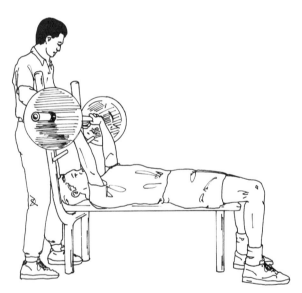

a

Preparation Phase

Spotting Keys

1. Alternated grip, inside partner's hands ___
2. Body positioning:
   a. Feet—hip width, 2 to 6 inches from bench ___
   b. Knees—slightly flexed ___
   c. Back—flat ___
3. React to "Okay" command ___
4. Assist with bar off supports ___
5. Guide bar to straight-elbow position ___
6. Release bar smoothly ___

Exercise Keys

1. Take an overhand grip, your hands at least shoulder-width apart ___
2. Body positioning, four points of contact. On bench—head, shoulders, buttocks; on floor—feet (straddle bench) ___
3. Eyes below edge of shelf ___
4. Signal "Okay" to spotter ___
5. Move bar off supports ___
6. Push to straight-elbow position over your chest ___
7. Keep your wrists directly above elbows throughout exercise ___

Downward Execution Phase

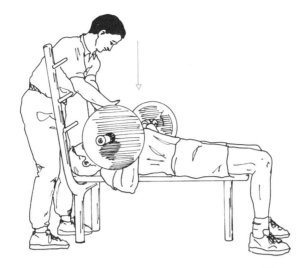

b

Spotting Keys

1. Hands closely follow downward bar movement ___
2. Assist only when necessary ___

Exercise Keys

1. Inhale while descending ___
2. Wrists straight ___
3. Slow, controlled movement ___
4. Bar touches chest near nipples ___
5. Pause as bar touches chest ___

Upward Execution Phase

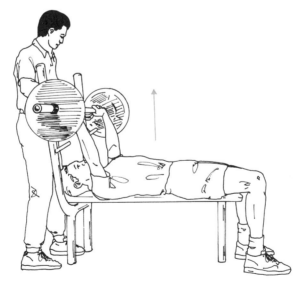

c

Spotting Keys

1. Hands closely lead bar movement ___
2. Watch for uneven arm extension ___
3. Watch for bar stopping or moving toward lifter's face ___

Exercise Keys

1. Push upward with your elbows extending evenly ___
2. Exhale during upward movement ___
3. Pause at straight-elbow position ___
4. Continue upward and downward movements until completion of the set ___
5. Signal "Okay" on the last repetition ___

Racking the Bar

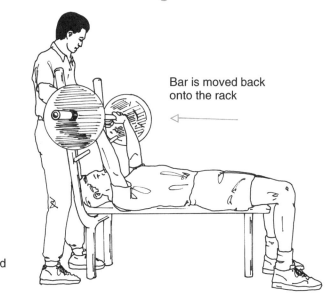

Bar is moved back
onto the rack

d

Spotting Keys

1. Grip bar (alternated grip) ___
2. Keep bar level ___
3. Guide to supports ___
4. Say "Okay" when racked ___

Exercise Keys

1. Keep elbows straight ___
2. Move bar to supports ___
3. Support until racked ___

FREE WEIGHT BENCH PRESS SUCCESS STOPPERS

Most errors associated with this exercise are a result of bar speed—you tend to lower and raise the bar too quickly. All of the errors listed here are made worse as the speed of the movement increases. Thus, the first step in correcting errors is to make sure that the bar is moving slowly; then attempt to make the specific corrective changes described for the errors that affect you.

Error	Correction
1. Your grip is not evenly spaced.	1. Evenly space your hands, using the markings on the bar and/or have your spotter help you locate a balanced position.
2. You are not properly positioned.	2. Position your eyes below the edge of the shelf and assume the four points of contact.
3. The bar's position on your chest is too high.	3. Watch the bar as it moves toward your chest, and concentrate on having it touch or nearly touch at your nipple area.
4. The bar bounces off your chest.	4. Control the bar's downward momentum, and pause briefly at the chest.

5. Your elbows extend unevenly.	5. Visually focus and concentrate on the arm that tends to lag behind.
6. You allow your wrists to hyperextend (roll back) about halfway up.	6. Concentrate on keeping your wrists in an extended (straight) position.
7. Your buttocks lift off the bench. This can cause the bar to move quickly toward your face, causing injury.	7. Lighten the load, and concentrate on keeping your buttocks in contact with the bench.
8. Bar hits the uprights.	8. You are positioned too close to the uprights. Slide down toward your feet a couple of inches.
9. When racking, you push the bar into the uprights.	9. Visually focus on and maintain control of the bar until it is safely in the rack.

Machine Exercises

If you have access to either a cam or multi- or single-unit machine, you may select either the bent-arm fly or the chest press exercise to develop your chest.

How to Perform the Bent-Arm Fly

Assume a sitting position with your back firmly against the back pad. Adjust the seat until your shoulders are aligned with the overhead cam. Sit erect, looking straight ahead, and place your forearms on the arm pads, with the elbows parallel to the shoulders. Grip each handle between your thumb and index finger (see Figure 3.2a).

While in this position, push with your forearms until the pads touch in front of your chest (see Figure 3.2b). Exhale as your elbows come together. Pause in this position, and then slowly return to the starting position while inhaling (see Figure 3.2c).

The bent-arm fly is different from the free weight bench press and the machine chest press concerning the muscle groups exercised. The triceps are involved in both the bench press and chest press but not in the bent-arm fly. The elbow is flexed in a 90-degree angle throughout the bent-arm fly exercise. The free weight equivalent to this is the dumbbell fly, which is described and demonstrated in Appendix A. This exercise is popular with body builders who want to continue to "pump" the chest muscles even though the triceps are fatigued.

FIGURE 3.2 **KEYS TO SUCCESS**

BENT-ARM FLY
(PEC DECK CHEST MACHINE)

a

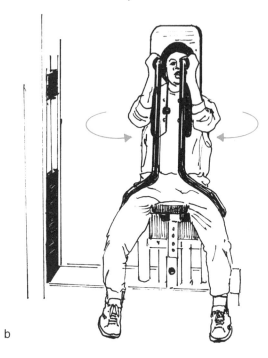

b

Preparation Phase

1. Head, shoulders, and back in contact with back pad __
2. Shoulders aligned with cam (while elbows are together) __
3. Grip each handle between thumb and index finger __
4. Forearms on arm pads __
5. Elbows shoulder high __

Forward Execution Phase

1. Push with forearms, not hands __
2. Head and torso stay on back pad __
3. Touch arm pads in front of chest __
4. Exhale as elbows come together __
5. Pause __

Backward Execution Phase

1. Return to starting position __
2. Inhale during return to starting position __
3. Pause __

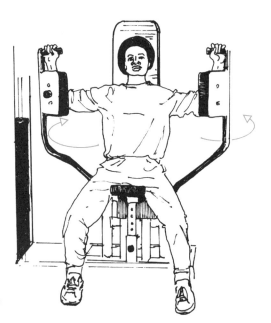

c

BENT-ARM FLY SUCCESS STOPPERS

Common errors in the bent-arm fly include body positioning on the equipment, incorrect head and torso positioning during the exercise, and pressing with the hands instead of the forearms.

Error	Correction
1. Your shoulders are not aligned with overhead cam.	1. Keep your torso in contact with back pad— if necessary, adjust seat.
2. Your forearms are not on arm pads.	2. Press firmly with your forearms and elbows—not your hands.
3. Your head and torso lean forward.	3. Keep your head and shoulders against back pad—lighten load if necessary.
4. You are pressing with hands.	4. Think, "Press elbows together."

How to Perform the Chest Press

Position yourself with head, shoulders, and buttocks in contact with the bench and feet flat on the floor about shoulder-width apart (four points of contact). Grip the bar handles with your hands shoulder-width apart, aligned with your nipples (see Figure 3.3a).

From this position, push to full elbow extension in a slow, controlled manner (see Figure 3.3b). Exhale through the sticking point of this exercise. Pause at full extension, then return to the starting position while inhaling (see Figure 3.3c). Caution! Be sure your head is at least 2 inches from the weight stack.

FIGURE
3.3 **KEYS TO SUCCESS**

CHEST PRESS
(MULTI- OR SINGLE-UNIT MACHINE)

Preparation Phase

1. Head, shoulders, buttocks stay on bench, feet on floor __
2. Grip slightly wider than shoulders __
3. Grip aligned with nipples on chest __

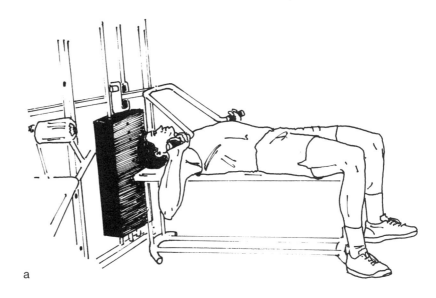

a

Upward Execution Phase

1. Push to full elbow extension ___
2. Exhale through the sticking point ___
3. Pause ___

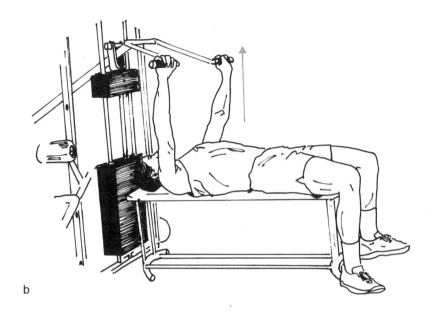

b

Downward Execution Phase

1. Return to starting position ___
2. Inhale during downward movement ___
3. Pause ___

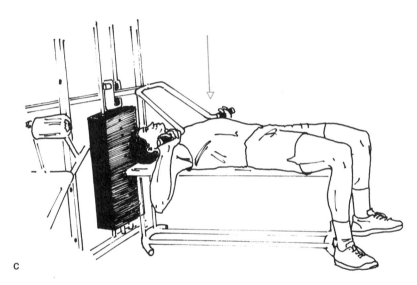

c

CHEST PRESS SUCCESS STOPPERS

Positioning the body too close to the weight stack, not executing each rep through the full range of motion, and allowing the weight-stack plates to bang against each other are common errors.

Error	Correction
1. Your body is positioned too close to the weight stack.	1. Dangerous—the selector key may strike your forehead. Slide toward your feet until there is approximately 2 inches of clearance.
2. The weight stack is stopped 2 or more inches above the rest of the weight stack.	2. Lower the weight stack to a point where it lightly touches the rest of the weight stack.

DEVELOPING THE CHEST

PRACTICE PROCEDURE DRILLS

1. Choose One Exercise

After reading about the characteristics and techniques involved in the three different exercises and the type of equipment required for each, you are ready to put what you have learned to use. Consider the availability of equipment and access to spotters in your situation, then select one of the following exercises to use in your program:

- Free weight bench press
- Bent-arm fly (cam machine)
- Chest press (multi- or single-unit weight machine)

Turn to Appendix C and copy your chest exercise choice onto the workout chart in the "Exercise" column.

Success Goal = 1 chest exercise selected and recorded ___

Success Check
- Consider availability of equipment ___
- Consider need for spotter ___
- Consider time available ___

2. Determine Trial and Warm-Up Loads

This practice procedure will ultimately answer the question, "How much weight or load should I use?" Using the coefficient associated with the chest exercise you selected and the formula below, determine the trial load. Then round your results to the nearest 5-pound increment, or to the closest weight-stack plate. Be sure to use the coefficient assigned to the exercise you selected. Use one-half of the amount determined for the trial load for your warm-up load in this exercise.

Trial Load Determination Formula CHEST						
Body weight	(Exercise)	×	Coefficient	=	Trial load	Warm-up load
Female						
BWT= _____	(FW-bench press)	×	.35	=	_____	_____
BWT= _____	(C-bent-arm fly)	×	.14	=	_____	_____
BWT= _____	(M-chest press)	×	.27	=	_____	_____
Male						
BWT= _____	(FW-bench press)	×	.60	=	_____	_____
BWT= _____	(C-bent-arm fly)	×	.30	=	_____	_____
BWT= _____	(M-chest press)	×	.55	=	_____	_____

BWT= body weight, FW = free weight, C = cam, and M = multi- or single-unit machine exercise.
Note. If you are a male who weighs more than 175 pounds (79.25 kg), then record your body weight as 175 (79.25 kg). If you are a female and weigh over 140 pounds (63.5 kg), then record your body weight as 140 (63.5 kg).

Success Goal = Record both trial and warm-up loads (These loads will be used in the next two procedures.) ___

Success Check
• Multiply your body weight by the correct coefficient ___
• Divide trial load by two for the warm-up load ___
• Round off to nearest weight stack for both the training and warm-up loads ___

3. Practice Proper Technique

In this procedure you are to perform 15 reps with the warm-up load determined in practice procedure 2.

Review the Keys to Success for proper grip and body positioning, and visualize the movement pattern through the full range of motion. Inhale when you are ready to execute the exercise, then perform the movement with a slow and controlled velocity, remembering to exhale through the sticking point. Ask a qualified person to observe and assess your performance in the basic techniques.

If you selected a machine exercise, move on to the next paragraph and disregard the spotting keys that follow.

Spotting the Free Weight Bench Press

If you selected the free weight bench press for developing your chest, you need a spotter, and you need to practice the skills of spotting. Identify a spotter with whom you will take turns when completing the Success Goals section. Instead of performing 15 reps in a continuous manner, rack the bar after each rep. There should be a handoff to begin each rep for 15 reps. Switch responsibilities so you and your partner both have a chance to develop the proper techniques that are required in performing and spotting the bench press. Ask a qualified person to observe and assess your performance in the basic techniques.

Success Goal =

a. Machine/free weight: 15 reps with calculated warm-up load ___

b. Free weight: 15 handoffs and rackings performed ___

Success Check

• All reps correctly performed ___

• Free weight: Handoffs and rackings correctly performed ___

4. Determine Training Load

This practice procedure will help you determine an appropriate training load designed to produce 12 to 15 reps. Use the calculated trial load from practice procedure 2 and perform as many reps as possible with this load. Make sure that the reps are correctly executed.

Success Goal = 12 to 15 reps with calculated trial load ___

Success Check

• Check for correct load ___

• Maintain good technique during each rep ___

If you executed 12 to 15 reps with the trial load, then your trial load becomes your training load. Record this as your "Training load" in Appendix C for this exercise. You are now ready to move on to the next chapter (Step 4).

5. Make Needed Load Adjustments

If you performed less than 12 reps with your trial load, it is too heavy and you should lighten the load. On the other hand, if you performed more than 15 reps, it is too light and you should increase the load. Use the formula and chart below as described in Step 2 (Figure 2.3) to make necessary adjustments.

Load Adjustment Chart	
Reps completed	Adjustment (in pounds)
<7	−15
8-9	−10
10-11	− 5
16-17	+ 5
18-19	+10
>20	+15

Determining the Training Load Formula				
Trial load (pounds)	+/−	Adjustment	=	Training load (pounds)
_____	+/−	_____	=	_____

Success Goal = Appropriate load adjustments are made ___

Success Check
• Check correct use of Load Adjustment Chart ___
• Record as the "Training load" in Appendix C ___

STEP 4

BACK EXERCISES: SELECTING ONE FOR YOUR PROGRAM

The bent over row using free weights, the rowing exercise using a cam machine, and the seated row using the low pulley on a multi- or single-purpose machine are excellent exercises to develop the upper back (rhomboid, trapezius, latissimus dorsi, teres major—see Appendix B, posterior view). These muscles work in opposition to those of the chest. Also developed are the back of the shoulders (posterior deltoid, infraspinatus, teres minor), the front of the upper arm (biceps brachii), and the back of the forearm (brachioradialis). This exercise should be performed as often as the bench press to keep the anterior and posterior upper body musculature in balance.

Free Weight Exercise

If you have access to free weights, you may select the bent over row exercise to develop your back. If you prefer working with machines, see the "Machine Exercises" section.

How to Perform the Bent Over Row

The preparation position begins with your feet shoulder-width apart and your shoulders slightly higher than your hips (10 to 30 degrees). Your back should be flat, abdominals contracted, elbows straight, knees slightly flexed, and eyes looking forward. Grasp the bar in a palms-down overhand grip with thumbs around the bar. Your hands should be evenly spaced 4 to 6 inches wider than shoulder width. Exhale as the bar nears the chest during the upward movement, and inhale during the downward movement.

The execution phase begins as the bar is pulled in a straight line upward. Pull in a slow, controlled manner until the bar touches your chest near the nipples (or, for women, just below your breasts). Your torso should remain straight and rigid throughout the exercise, with no bouncing or jerking. When the bar is touching your chest, pause momentarily in this position before beginning the downward movement. Slowly lower the bar in a straight line to the starting position without letting the weight touch the floor or bounce at the bottom. Be sure to keep the knees slightly flexed during the upward and downward movements to avoid putting undue stress on the lower back. Figure 4.1, a-c, shows the exercise Keys to Success for executing the bent over row.

Special Caution

Although this is considered to be one of the best exercises for the upper back, it is also one that is often performed with bad technique or modified more than usual. Do not be lulled into using heavier weights, thinking that it will increase your strength faster, or because you are trying to impress your friends and other people in the weight room. Attempting to lift too much weight leads to bad technique and possible injury. One of the easiest mistakes you can make is to use a heavier weight than you can handle. Another is to pull upward, simultaneously lifting with your legs and lower back and then to quickly drop your chest to make contact with the bar. This practice of quickly dropping your chest puts the lower back at great stress and in danger of possible injury, and does little for improvement of the upper back.

This exercise is usually modified by placing the forehead on something to brace the back and to use the neck to support some of the weight. There are arguments for and against this practice, but the authors of this text are against using a head support for the following reasons. First, if you need to use this technique you are probably attempting to use too much weight and might continue this practice until injuring the vertebrae in your neck. Second, if the proper stance is taken and technique followed, as previously explained, the extra support is not needed. Third, if the lower back will not support this movement without additional support, then you should concentrate on strengthening that area.

FIGURE
4.1

KEYS TO SUCCESS

FREE WEIGHT BENT OVER ROW

Preparation Phase

1. Overhand grip, hands at least shoulder-width apart ___
2. Shoulders higher than hips ___
3. Lower back flat ___
4. Elbows straight ___
5. Knees slightly flexed ___
6. Head up, facing forward ___

a

Upward Execution Phase

1. Pull bar straight up, slowly ___
2. Pause momentarily as bar touches chest ___
3. Touch chest near nipples ___
4. Keep torso rigid ___
5. Exhale as bar nears chest ___

b

Downward Execution Phase

1. Slowly lower bar straight down ___
2. Do not bounce or jerk weight at bottom ___
3. Do not allow weight to touch floor ___
4. Inhale during downward movement ___
5. Continue upward and downward movements until set is completed ___

c

FREE WEIGHT BENT OVER ROW SUCCESS STOPPERS

Most errors associated with the bent over row derive from using too much weight and from not maintaining the proper body position. When too much weight is used, the back muscles are not able to pull the bar all the way to the chest. This reduces the extent to which the back muscles can be worked and developed. You will tend to jerk the bar, using momentum to get the bar to the chest, then let it free-fall back to the starting position. Avoiding the temptation of using heavy loads will enable you to more effectively work the back muscles because the bar is being pulled all the way to the chest. It is also important to establish and maintain the proper body position. A correct shoulder-to-back position places the back muscles in an ideal alignment for strengthening and reduces the likelihood of injury to the lower back.

Error	Correction
1. The bar does not touch your chest.	1. Reduce the weight on the bar and concentrate on touching your chest with the bar.
2. Your shoulders are lower than your hips.	2. Elevate your shoulders 10 to 30 degrees above your hips.
3. Your knees are locked out.	3. Flex your knees slightly to reduce stress on your lower back.
4. Your upper back is rounded.	4. Lift your head up and look straight forward.
5. Your upper torso is not stable and moves up and down.	5. Use a mirror to watch and maintain the proper position, or have someone place their hand on your upper back.
6. On the upward movement you quickly drop your chest to make contact with the bar.	6. If you cannot pull the bar to your chest with strict form you should lighten the weight.

Machine Exercises

If you have access to either a cam or multi- or single-unit machine, you may select either the rowing or the seated row exercise to develop your back.

How to Perform the Rowing Exercise

Assume a sitting position with your back toward the weight stack. Sit erect, looking straight ahead, and place your upper arms between the pads with your forearms crossed (see Figure 4.2, a-c). While maintaining this position, pull your arms in a rowing movement as far back as possible. Exhale at this time. Pause and then return slowly to the starting position while inhaling. Keep your forearms parallel to the floor at all times.

FIGURE 4.2

KEYS TO SUCCESS

ROWING EXERCISE
(CAM ROWING MACHINE)

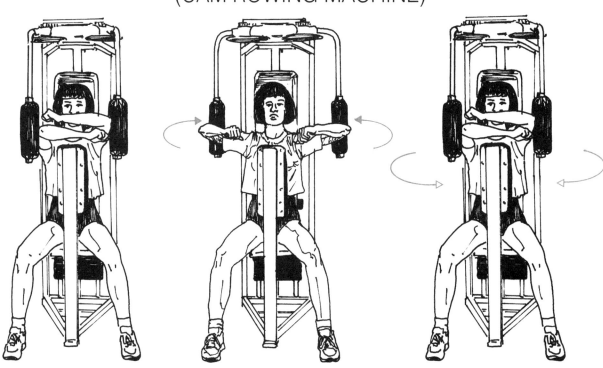

a

b

c

Preparation Phase

1. Sit with back toward weight stack ___
2. Place upper arms between pads and cross forearms ___

Backward Execution Phase

1. Pull arms in a rowing movement as far back as possible ___
2. Keep forearms parallel to the floor at all times ___
3. Exhale while pulling ___
4. Pause ___

Forward Execution Phase

1. Return slowly to starting position ___
2. Inhale while returning to starting position ___

ROWING EXERCISE SUCCESS STOPPERS

Common errors in this exercise include not performing it throughout the full range of movement and not maintaining the proper arm position.

Error	Correction
1. You do not complete full range of motion.	1. Bring your elbows back until they form a straight line with each other.
2. Your forearms are not parallel to the floor.	2. Keep your palms facing the floor at all times.

How to Perform the Seated Row

At the low pulley station, assume a seated position with your knees slightly flexed. Keep your torso erect, with your lower back and abdominal muscles contracted. Take a grip, with palms facing inward. Maintain this position while pulling the bar slowly and smoothly to your chest. Exhale as the bar nears your chest. Pause, then return to the starting position while inhaling. Your upper torso should not be allowed to move back and forth (see Figure 4.3, a-c).

FIGURE
4.3

KEYS TO SUCCESS

SEATED ROW
(ROWING STATION—MULTI- OR SINGLE-UNIT MACHINE)

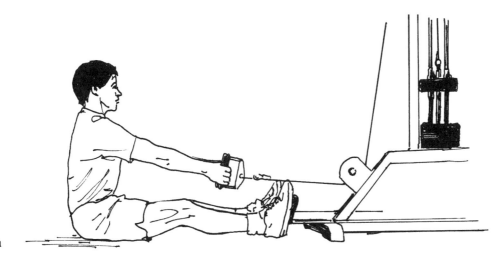

a

Preparation Phase

1. Assume a seated position, knees slightly flexed ___
2. Keep upper torso erect, lower back flat ___
3. Take a palms facing inward grip ___

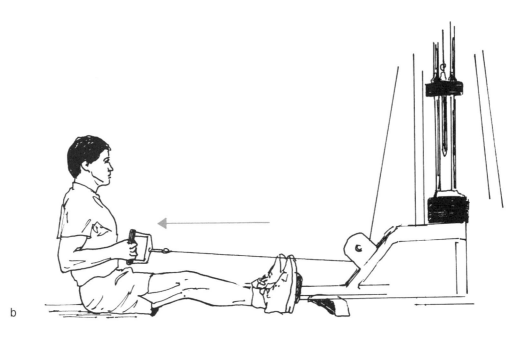

b

Backward Execution Phase

1. Pull bar slowly and smoothly to chest ___
2. Do not use torso movements to pull weight ___
3. Exhale as bar nears chest ___
4. Pause ___

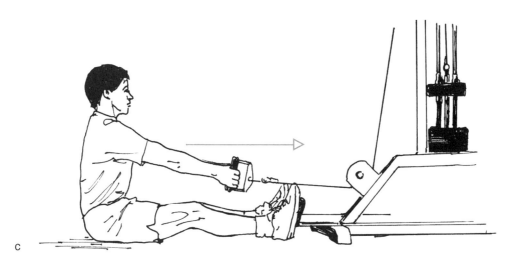

c

Forward Execution Phase

1. Return to starting position ___
2. Inhale during the return ___

SEATED ROW SUCCESS STOPPERS

The most common error observed in the seated row exercise is allowing the upper body to move forward and backward instead of remaining erect throughout the exercise. When this happens, the lower back muscles become involved in pulling. This compromises the benefit to the upper back muscles for which this exercise was designed and selected.

Error	Correction
1. Your knees are not flexed.	1. Make sure your knees are slightly flexed to decrease pressure on your lower back.
2. Your torso is not erect.	2. Keep your torso erect by contracting your abdominal and lower back muscles.
3. You allow the weight plate to fall quickly to the weight stack.	3. Pause at your chest—then slowly return the bar to the starting position.
4. You use torso movement to pull the bar to your chest.	4. Keep your upper torso rigid—lighten the weight if necessary.

DEVELOPING THE BACK

PRACTICE PROCEDURE DRILLS

1. Choose One Exercise

After reading about the characteristics and techniques of the three different exercises and the type of equipment required for each, you are ready to put what you have learned to use. Consider the availability of equipment in your situation, then select one of the following exercises to use in your program.

- Free weight bent over row
- Rowing exercise (cam rowing machine)
- Seated row (multi- or single-unit weight machine)

Please turn to Appendix C and copy your back exercise choice onto the workout chart in the "Exercise" column.

Success Goal = 1 back exercise selected ___

Success Check
- Consider availability of equipment ___
- Consider time available ___

2. Determine Trial and Warm-Up Loads

This practice procedure will answer the question, "How much weight or load should I use?" Using the coefficient associated with the back exercise you selected, and the formula below, determine the trial load. Then round off your results to the nearest 5-pound increment or to the closest weight-stack plate. Be sure to use the coefficient assigned to the exercise you selected. Use one-half of the amount determined for the trial load for your warm-up load in this exercise.

Trial Load Determination Formula BACK						
Body weight	(Exercise)	$\times$	Coefficient	$=$	Trial load	Warm-up load
Female						
BWT=_____	(FW-bent over row)	$\times$	.35	$=$	_____	_____
BWT=_____	(C-rowing exercise)	$\times$	.20	$=$	_____	_____
BWT=_____	(M-chest press)	$\times$	.25	$=$	_____	_____
Male						
BWT=_____	(FW-bent over row)	$\times$	.45	$=$	_____	_____
BWT=_____	(C-rowing exercise)	$\times$	.40	$=$	_____	_____
BWT=_____	(M-seated row)	$\times$	.45	$=$	_____	_____

BWT= body weight, FW = free weight, C = cam, and M = multi- or single-unit machine exercise.
Note. If you are a male who weighs more than 175 pounds (79.25 kg), then record your body weight as 175 (79.25 kg). If you are a female and weigh over 140 pounds (63.5 kg), then record your body weight as 140 (63.5 kg).

Success Goal = Record both trial and warm-up loads (These loads will be used in the next two procedures.) ___

Success Check
• Multiply your body weight by the correct coefficient ___
• Divide trial load by two for the warm-up load ___
• Round off to nearest weight stack for both the training and warm-up loads ___

3. Practice Proper Technique

In this procedure you are to perform 15 reps with the warm-up load determined in practice procedure 2.

Review the Keys to Success for proper grip and body positioning, and visualize the movement pattern through the full range of motion. Inhale when you are ready to execute the exercise, then perform the movement with a slow and controlled velocity, remembering to exhale through the sticking point. Ask a qualified person to observe and assess your performance in the basic techniques.

Success Goal = 15 reps with calculated warm-up load ___

Success Check
• Check movement pattern ___
• Check velocity ___
• Check breathing ___

4. Determine Training Load

This practice procedure will help you determine an appropriate training load that is designed to produce 12 to 15 reps. Use the calculated trial load from practice procedure 2 and perform as many reps as possible with this load. Make sure that all reps are correctly executed. If you are executing the free weight bent over row, also check that your hips are lower than your back, and that the bar touches on or near the nipples.

Success Goal = 12 to 15 reps with calculated trial load ___

Success Check
• Check for correct load ___
• Maintain good technique during each rep ___

If you executed 12 to 15 reps with your trial load, then your trial load becomes your training load. Record this as your "Training load" in Appendix C for this exercise. You are now ready to move on to the next chapter (Step 5).

5. Make Needed Load Adjustments

If you did not perform 12 reps with your trial load, it is too heavy and you should lighten the load. On the other hand, if you performed more than 15 reps, it is too light and you should increase the load. Use the formula and chart below as described in Step 2 (Figure 2.3) to make necessary adjustments.

Load Adjustment Chart	
Reps completed	Adjustment (in pounds)
<7	−15
8-9	−10
10-11	− 5
16-17	+ 5
18-19	+10
>20	+15

Determining the Training Load Formula				
Trial load (pounds)	+/−	Adjustment	=	Training load (pounds)
_____	+/−	_____	=	_____

Success Goal = Appropriate load adjustments are made ___

Success Check
• Check correct use of Load Adjustment Chart ___
• Record as the "Training load" in Appendix C ___

STEP 5

SHOULDER EXERCISES: SELECTING ONE FOR YOUR PROGRAM

Overhead pressing exercises using free weights, a pulley/pivot machine, or a cam machine are excellent for developing the front and middle of the shoulder (anterior and middle heads of the deltoid shown in Appendix B, posterior view). The back of the upper arm (triceps) is also developed. These exercises contribute to shoulder-joint stabilization and muscle padding for protection, as well as to balanced muscular development of the chest and upper back. The free weight standing press, also called the military press, is generally considered to be the best combined shoulder and arm exercise.

Free Weight Exercise

If you have access to free weights, you may select the standing press exercise to develop your shoulders. If you prefer working with machines, see the "Machine Exercise" section.

How to Perform the Free Weight Standing Press

Preparation for performing this exercise involves placing the bar on a squat rack or a set of supports at shoulder height. If racks or supports are not available, you must lift the bar from the floor, utilizing the techniques presented in Step 2. Grasp the bar in an overhand grip, with your hands equidistant from the center of the bar and slightly more than shoulder-width apart. Hold your wrists firmly in a slightly extended position with elbows under the bar. The bar should be resting on your shoulders, clavicle (collarbone), and hands (see Figure 5.1a).

Push the bar upward in a straight line above the shoulders at a slow to moderate speed, until your elbows are extended (see Figure 5.1b). You will need to move your head slightly backward as the bar starts moving off of and returning to the shoulders. Otherwise the head should be maintained in an upright position throughout this exercise. Avoid leaning back or hyperextending the spine (exaggerating the lower back curvature) during the press. Pause momentarily at the top of this exercise, then lower the bar slowly to the ready position (see Figure 5.1c). Do not bounce the bar on your upper chest. You should inhale as you lower the bar and exhale as the bar passes through the sticking point on ascent. Caution! Be very careful not to hold your breath through the sticking point because this may cause you to pass out. If you must lower the bar to the floor after completing the exercise, use the shoulder-to-floor lowering techniques presented in Step 2.

FIGURE
5.1

KEYS TO SUCCESS

FREE WEIGHT STANDING PRESS

Preparation Phase

Exercise Keys

1. Overhand grip, evenly spaced, shoulder-width or slightly wider ___
2. Head upright, facing forward ___
3. Elbows under bar, wrists extended ___
4. Bar resting in hands on shoulders and clavicle ___

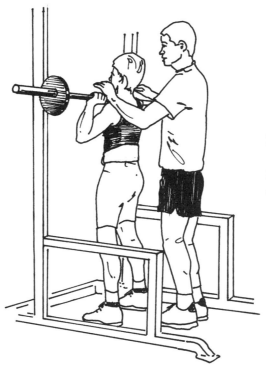

Spotting Keys

1. Stand directly behind partner ___
2. Stand as close as possible without touching ___
3. Eyes watching bar ___
4. Feet shoulder-width apart ___

a

Upward Execution Phase

Exercise Keys

1. Push bar straight up ___
2. Keep your back flat and erect ___
3. Caution—exhale through sticking point ___
4. Pause at top ___

Spotting Keys

1. Hands close to bar, tracking upward bar movement ___
2. Assist only if necessary ___
3. Caution partner not to lean back and/or hold breath ___

b

Downward Execution Phase

Exercise Keys

1. Lower bar slowly ___
2. Do not bounce bar off upper chest ___
3. Inhale on descent ___

Spotting Keys

1. Hands close to bar, tracking downward bar movement ___
2. Watch for excessive bar speed ___
3. Caution partner not to bounce bar off upper chest ___

c

Racking the Bar

Exercise Keys

1. Walk forward until bar contacts rack ___
2. Bend the knees to place the bar in the rack ___
3. Never lean forward to rack bar ___

Spotting Keys

1. Walk with partner until bar is racked ___
2. Tell your partner when the bar is safely racked ___

d

FREE WEIGHT STANDING PRESS SUCCESS STOPPERS

Of the errors commonly seen when observing the standing press, leaning back too far is the most common. This should be avoided because it places a lot of stress on the lower back. This and other common errors, and suggestions for correcting them, are presented next.

Error	Correction
1. Your grip is too wide.	1. Evenly space your hands using the markings on the bar for reference.
2. Your torso is leaning back too far.	2. This typically occurs at the bar's sticking point. Think, "Torso, head, and bar form a straight line."
3. Your eyes are closed.	3. Concentrate on focusing on some object straight ahead, especially when reaching the sticking point.
4. You hold your breath.	4. Remember to begin exhaling as the bar reaches the sticking point.
5. Your arms are extended unevenly.	5. Keep both of your arms extending in unison by visually focusing and concentrating on the arm that lags behind.
6. You start the bar upward with a knee kick (flexion, then quick extension).	6. Start with your knees in a fully extended position, and keep them that way throughout the upward and downward movements.

Machine Exercises

If you have access to either a cam or multi- or single-unit machine, you may select either of the seated press exercises to develop your shoulders.

How to Perform the Seated Press (Weight Machine)

Assume an erect sitting position on the stool so that the front of your shoulders are directly below the handles. Take a palms-forward grip approximately shoulder-width apart. Push the handles upward until your elbows extend completely. Keep your shoulders directly under the handles throughout the exercise, and keep your lower back flat by statically contracting the muscles of your lower back and abdominal area. Exhale as your elbows near the fully extended (sticking point) position. Pause when the elbows are fully extended, then slowly return to the starting position (see Figure 5.2, a-c).

FIGURE
5.2 **KEYS TO SUCCESS**

SEATED PRESS
(MULTI- OR SINGLE-UNIT WEIGHT MACHINE)

Preparation Phase

1. Assume a seated position on a stool so that the front of shoulders are directly below the handles ___
2. Palms-forward grip approximately shoulder-width apart ___
3. Shoulders should stay directly under handles ___
4. Keep lower back flat ___

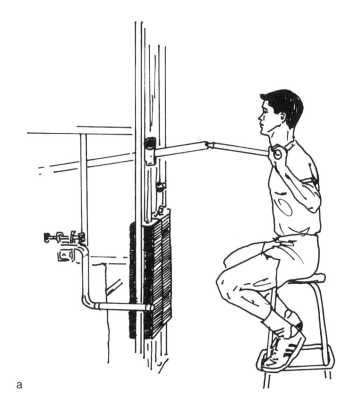

a

Upward Execution Phase

1. Push up to complete extension ___
2. Exhale during upward movement ___
3. Pause ___

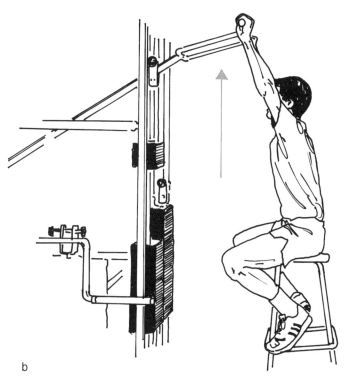

b

Downward Execution Phase

1. Return to starting position ___
2. Inhale on downward movement ___

c

SEATED PRESS (WEIGHT MACHINE) SUCCESS STOPPERS

The most common errors observed when this exercise is performed are hyperextending (excessively arching) the lower back and not lowering the handles to shoulder level. Hyperextending the lower back subjects it to a lot of stress, and not lowering the handles reduces the range through which the shoulder muscles work, thus minimizing their development. These and other commonly observed errors, and suggestions for correcting them, are discussed next.

Error	Correction
1. You arch your back excessively when reaching the sticking point.	1. Keep your back flat by contracting your abdominal and lower back muscles. Think, "Head, torso, and buttocks form a straight line."
2. You hold your breath.	2. Begin exhaling as the handles reach the sticking point.
3. You don't lower the handles to shoulder level.	3. Try to lower the handles enough to have the weight plate lightly touch (not bang) the weight stack.
4. The weight plates bang against each other.	4. Control the handles' downward momentum, and pause at shoulder level before pushing upward.

How to Perform the Shoulder Press (Cam Machine)

Position yourself on the seat with your back against the pad and your shoulders aligned under the handles. Grasp the handles with a palms-inward grip. From this position push to full elbow extension in a slow, controlled manner (see Figure 5.3, a-c). Exhale when passing through the sticking point. Pause at full extension, then return to the starting position while inhaling.

FIGURE 5.3

KEYS TO SUCCESS

SHOULDER PRESS
(CAM MACHINE)

a

Preparation Phase

1. Assume a seated position against pad ___
2. Take a palms-inward grip ___

b

Upward Execution Phase

1. Push up to complete extension ___
2. Elbows directly under wrists ___
3. Exhale through sticking point of upward movement ___
4. Pause ___

c

Downward Execution Phase

1. Return to starting position ___
2. Inhale while lowering weight to starting position ___

SHOULDER PRESS (CAM MACHINE) SUCCESS STOPPERS

The most common error observed during this exercise is the tendency to arch the lower back when the sticking point is reached. The back should be kept flat against the pad because the arched back position inappropriately stresses the lower back. This error and others common to the shoulder press exercise, along with suggestions for correction, are presented next.

Error	Correction
1. Your lower back is not against the pad.	1. Slide back on the seat until your lower back is against the pad.
2. Your lower back arches when the sticking point is reached.	2. Concentrate on keeping your buttocks and lower back pressed against the pad.
3. You hold your breath during the sticking point.	3. Begin exhaling as the bar nears the extended-elbow position.

DEVELOPING THE SHOULDERS

PRACTICE PROCEDURE DRILLS

1. Choose One Exercise

After reading about the characteristics and techniques of the three different exercises and the type of equipment required for each, you are ready to put this information to use. Consider the availability of equipment and your situation, then select one of the following exercises to use in your program.

- Free weight standing press
- Seated press (multi- or single-unit weight machine)
- Shoulder press (cam machine)

Please turn to Appendix C and copy your shoulder exercise choice onto the workout chart.

Success Goal = 1 shoulder exercise selected ___

Success Check
- Consider availability of equipment ___
- Consider need for spotter ___
- Consider time available ___

2. Determine Trial and Warm-Up Loads

The next practice procedure answers the question, "How much weight or load should I use?" Using the coefficient associated with the shoulder exercise you selected and the formula below, determine the trial load. Then round your results to the nearest 5-pound increment or to the closest weight-stack plate. Use one-half of the amount determined for the trial load for your warm-up load in this exercise.

Trial Load Determination Formula SHOULDERS						
Body weight	(Exercise)	×	Coefficient	=	Trial load	Warm-up load
Female						
BWT= _____	(FW-Standing press)	×	.22	=	_____	_____
BWT= _____	(C-seated press)	×	.15	=	_____	_____
BWT= _____	(M-shoulder press)	×	.25	=	_____	_____
Male						
BWT= _____	(FW-Standing press)	×	.38	=	_____	_____
BWT= _____	(C-seated press)	×	.35	=	_____	_____
BWT= _____	(M-shoulder press)	×	.40	=	_____	_____

BWT= body weight, FW = free weight, C = cam, and M = multi- or single-unit machine exercise.
Note. If you are a male who weighs more than 175 pounds (79.25 kg), then record your body weight as 175 (79.25 kg). If you are a female and weigh over 140 pounds (63.5 kg), then record your body weight as 140 (63.5 kg).

Success Goal = Record both trial and warm-up loads (These loads will be used in the next two procedures.) ___

Success Check
• Multiply your body weight by the correct coefficient ___
• Divide trial load by two for the warm-up load ___
• Round off to nearest weight stack for both the training and warm-up loads ___

3. Practice Proper Technique

In this procedure you are to perform 15 reps with the warm-up load determined in practice procedure 2. Focus on the following techniques.

Review the Keys to Success for proper grip and body positioning, and visualize the movement pattern through the full range of motion. Inhale when you are ready to execute the exercise, then perform the movement with a slow and controlled velocity, remembering to exhale through the sticking point. Ask a qualified person to observe and assess your performance in the basic techniques.

If you selected a machine exercise, move on to the next paragraph and disregard the spotting keys that follow.

Spotting the Free Weight Standing Press

If you selected the free weight standing press for developing your shoulders, you need a spotter, and you need to practice the skills of spotting. Identify a spotter and take turns when completing the Success Goals section. Switch responsibilities so you and your partner both have a chance to develop the proper techniques that are required in performing and spotting the free weight standing press. Ask a qualified person to observe and assess your performance in the basic techniques.

Success Goal = 15 reps with calculated warm-up load ___

Success Check
• All reps correctly performed ___

4. Determine Training Load

This practice procedure will help you determine an appropriate training load designed to produce 12 to 15 reps. Use the calculated trial load from practice procedure 2 and perform as many reps as possible with this load.

Success Goal = 12 to 15 reps with calculated trial load ___

Success Check
• Check for correct load ___
• Maintain good technique during each rep ___

If you executed 12 to 15 reps with your trial load, then your trial load becomes your training load. Record this as your "Training load" in Appendix C for this exercise. You are now ready to move on to the next chapter (Step 6).

5. Make Needed Load Adjustments

If you did not complete 12 reps with your trial load, it is too heavy and you should lighten the load. On the other hand, if you performed more than 15 reps, it is too light and you should increase the load. Use the formula and chart below as described in Step 2 (Figure 2.3) to make the necessary adjustments.

Load Adjustment Chart	
Reps completed	Adjustment (in pounds)
<7	−15
8-9	−10
10-11	− 5
16-17	+ 5
18-19	+10
>20	+15

Determining the Training Load Formula				
Trial load (pounds)	+/−	Adjustment	=	Training load (pounds)
_____	+/−	_____	=	_____

Success Goal = Appropriate load adjustments are made ___

Success Check
- Check correct use of Load Adjustment Chart ___
- Record as the "Training load" in Appendix C ___

STEP 6

UPPER ARM EXERCISES: SELECTING TWO FOR YOUR PROGRAM

Exercises that develop the upper arm are very popular, especially with beginning weight trainers and body builders. These muscles respond quickly when properly trained, and changes in this muscle area are typically noticed more and sooner than changes in other body parts. The anterior and posterior portions of the upper arm are commonly known as the biceps (the traditional "show me your muscle" muscle admired by many) and the triceps, respectively.

The free weight biceps curl, the preacher curl using the cam-type machine, and the low pulley biceps curl using a single- or multi-purpose weight machine are ideal exercises to develop the front of the upper arm (biceps muscles shown in Appendix B, anterior view). Muscles in the front of the forearm (anterior forearm muscles) are also developed.

The free weight triceps extension, the triceps extension using the cam machine, and the press-down exercise on a multi- or single-unit weight machine are excellent exercises for developing the back of the upper arm (triceps, shown in Appendix B, posterior view). When properly developed, the biceps and triceps muscles contribute to elbow joint stabilization and, to a lesser extent, shoulder stabilization (long head of both biceps and triceps). Development of these muscles contributes to activities that require pulling (biceps), or pushing or throwing (triceps), motions.

Free Weight Exercises

If you have access to free weights, you may select the biceps curl exercise and the triceps extension exercise to develop your upper arm. If you prefer working with machines, see the "Machine Exercises" section.

How to Perform the Free Weight Biceps Curl

The preparation position involves gripping the bar underhand with the hands about shoulder-width apart. Your hands should be evenly spaced. Hold your upper arms against your ribs and perpendicular to the floor. Your elbows should be fully extended.

The bar should be touching the front of your thighs in this position. Your back should be straight, your eyes looking straight ahead. Your knees should be slightly flexed to reduce the stress on the lower back.

The execution phase begins by pulling the bar upward toward your shoulders, keeping your elbows and upper arms perpendicular to the floor and close to your sides. Avoid allowing your elbows and upper arms to move back or out to the sides. Your body must remain straight and erect throughout the exercise; no rocking, swinging, or jerking should occur. Begin to exhale as the bar nears your shoulders (sticking point). After flexing the elbows as far as possible, inhale as you slowly lower the bar back to your thighs (see Figure 6.1, a-c). Your elbows should be fully extended and there should be a momentary pause at the thighs between each rep.

FIGURE 6.1 **KEYS TO SUCCESS**

FREE WEIGHT BICEPS CURL

a

b

c

Preparation Phase

1. Underhand grip, hands shoulder-width apart ___
2. Torso erect ___
3. Head up, facing forward ___
4. Upper arms against ribs, elbows extended ___
5. Bar touching front of thighs ___

Upward Execution Phase

1. Keep upper arms stationary ___
2. Keep elbows close to body ___
3. Curl bar to shoulders ___
4. Do not rock, jerk, or swing body ___
5. Begin to exhale as bar nears shoulders ___

Downward Execution Phase

1. Inhale during downward movement ___
2. Lower bar slowly to thighs ___
3. Keep elbows close to sides ___
4. Extend arms completely ___

FREE WEIGHT BICEPS CURL SUCCESS STOPPERS

The free weight biceps curl is probably one of the easiest exercises to perform, but unfortunately it is probably the one that is most often performed incorrectly. The most common errors are not extending the elbows completely between reps, leaning backward, and using momentum to complete the reps.

Error	Correction
1. Your elbows are slightly flexed in the preparatory position.	1. Stand erect, with your shoulders back and your elbows extended.
2. Your upper arms move backward.	2. Squeeze the inside of your upper arms against your ribs.
3. You allow your wrists to hyperextend (roll back).	3. Concentrate on keeping your wrists straight or slightly flexed.
4. You use momentum to complete the rep.	4. Keep your upper body erect. If this problem persists, stand with your back against the wall.
5. Your elbows do not extend completely between reps.	5. Pause long enough to watch your elbows extend before curling the bar upward.

How to Perform the Preacher Curl

For this biceps exercise option, assume a sitting position with the chest against the pad. Place your elbows on the pad in line with the axes of the cams. Adjust the seat so that your elbows are slightly lower than your shoulders. Grasp the bar in an underhand grip. Begin the exercise at full elbow extension. Curl the bar upward as far as possible, pausing briefly at the top position. Exhale as the bar passes through the sticking point. Inhale as you slowly lower the bar to the starting position, being careful not to allow the elbows to hyperextend (see Figure 6.2, a-c).

FIGURE
6.2 **KEYS TO SUCCESS**

PREACHER CURL
(CAM MACHINE)

Preparation Phase

1. Sit with chest against the pad __
2. Place elbows on pad in line with axis of cam __
3. Adjust seat so elbows are slightly lower than shoulders __
4. Grasp bar with an underhand grip __

a

Upward Execution Phase

1. Curl upward as far as possible __
2. Exhale through the sticking point __

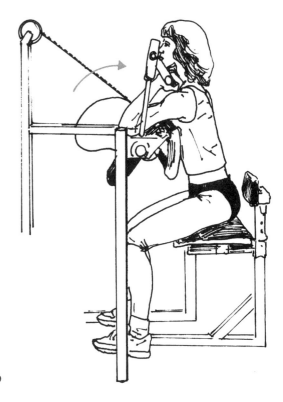

b

Downward Execution Phase

1. Inhale while slowly lowering the bar to starting position ___
2. Do not allow elbows to hyperextend ___

c

PREACHER CURL SUCCESS STOPPERS

Common errors in this exercise include not keeping the entire upper arm on the pad, and not pausing at the extended-elbow position. These and other commonly observed errors, and corrections for them, are presented next.

Error	Correction
1. Your elbows are not in line with the axis of the cam.	1. Reposition arms.
2. Your elbows are flexed at the start of the exercise.	2. Start the exercise with your elbows fully extended.
3. You do not go through the full range of motion.	3. Curl upward until your hands almost touch your shoulders, and lower until the elbows are fully extended.
4. You allow weights to drop quickly.	4. Slowly lower the bar, being careful not to hyperextend your elbows.
5. You do not breathe properly.	5. Exhale when passing through the sticking point upward; inhale when lowering the bar.
6. You use upper torso movement to complete curl.	6. Keep chest against pad and elbows in line with cam.

How to Perform the Low Pulley Biceps Curl

Assume a position facing the weight machine with your feet approximately 18 inches from it. Keep your torso erect, with your head up and looking forward. Your knees should be slightly flexed, your shoulders leaning back. Grasp the bar in an underhand grip and begin the exercise with the bar touching the front of the thighs and your elbows fully extended. Curl the bar until it almost touches your shoulders. Avoid allowing your upper arms to move backward or out to the sides. Exhale as you pass through the sticking point and inhale while lowering the bar (see Figure 6.3, a-c).

FIGURE 6.3

KEYS TO SUCCESS

LOW PULLEY BICEPS CURL
(MULTI- OR SINGLE-UNIT WEIGHT MACHINE)

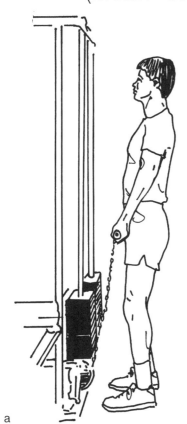 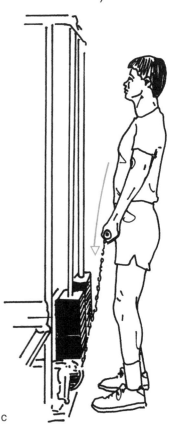

a   b   c

Preparation Phase

1. Torso erect ___
2. Knees slightly flexed ___
3. Head up, looking forward, shoulders back ___
4. Underhand grip ___
5. Extend elbows fully ___
6. Bar resting on the thighs ___

Upward Execution Phase

1. Pull bar to shoulder level ___
2. Keep upper arms stationary ___
3. Exhale as bar nears shoulders ___
4. Pause ___

Downward Execution Phase

1. Slowly lower bar to starting position ___
2. Keep head up, looking forward, shoulders back ___
3. Inhale when lowering bar ___

LOW PULLEY BICEPS CURL SUCCESS STOPPERS

The error most often observed in the low pulley biceps curl is not allowing the elbows to fully extend at the beginning of each repetition. This and other errors common to this exercise, and corrections for them, are presented next.

Error	Correction
1. Your torso leans forward.	1. Keep your torso erect and shoulders leaning back.
2. Your knees are locked out.	2. As you pull the bar upward, you will be pulled forward. Keep your knees slightly flexed and shoulders leaning back.
3. Your head is down, looking at the floor, and your shoulders forward.	3. Keep your head up, looking slightly above eye level, with your shoulders pulled back and chest out.
4. Your elbows are flexed at the start.	4. Fully extend your elbows before starting and between each rep.
5. You do not go through full range of motion.	5. Raise the bar until it almost touches your shoulder, and fully extend your elbows.
6. You allow the weight plates to drop quickly to the weight stack.	6. Slowly lower the weight, allowing the weight plate to touch, not bang, against the weight stack.

How to Perform the Free Weight Triceps Extension

The preparation position involves holding the bar in a narrow overhand grip with hands approximately 6 inches apart. Use the fundamental lifting techniques presented in Step 2 to take the bar from the floor to the shoulders, and those in Step 5 to press the bar to a fully extended position overhead.

The execution phase begins by lowering the bar in a slow, controlled manner behind your head to shoulder level by flexing the elbows. The upper arms maintain a vertical position as the bar is lowered with elbows pointing straight up.

From a fully flexed position, push the bar back to fully extended position. During the upward movement, your elbows will have a tendency to move forward and bow out. Keep your upper arms close to your ears and your elbows pointing straight up. You should exhale through the sticking point, which occurs as the bar approaches the top position. Inhale while the bar is being lowered. Do not move the legs or body in any way to assist in moving the bar upward (see Figure 6.4, a-c).

FIGURE
6.4 **KEYS TO SUCCESS**

FREE WEIGHT TRICEPS EXTENSION

a　　　　　　　　　　　b　　　　　　　　　　　c

Preparation Phase

1. Overhand grip, hands 6 inches apart ___
2. Torso erect ___
3. Head up, facing forward ___
4. Feet shoulder-width apart ___
5. Elbows close to ears and pointing straight up ___

Downward Execution Phase

1. Lower bar behind head to top of shoulders ___
2. Keep elbows pointed up ___
3. Control downward movement ___
4. Inhale as bar is lowered ___

Upward Execution Phase

1. Push bar to full extension ___
2. Keep elbows back, close to ears, and pointing upward ___
3. Exhale as bar passes through sticking point ___

FREE WEIGHT TRICEPS EXTENSION SUCCESS STOPPERS

Most errors associated with the triceps extension involve moving the upper arms out of position. When using free weights, your elbows will tend to move forward and bow out during the upward phase. You should concentrate on keeping your elbows close to the ears and pointing them straight up. This and other common errors, and corrections for them, are described next.

Error	Correction
1. Your hands are too far apart.	1. Space your hands no more than 6 inches apart.
2. You drop the bar instead of lowering it.	2. Think "Lower" not "Drop." Control the bar's downward momentum, and pause at shoulder level before pushing upward.
3. Your elbows move forward during upward phase.	3. Concentrate on keeping your elbows pointing straight up.
4. Your elbows bow out away from your head.	4. Concentrate on keeping your upper arms close to your ears.
5. You do not lower the bar to the top of your shoulders.	5. Perform exercise in front of mirror and lower the bar to shoulder level during each rep.

Machine Exercises

If you have access to either a cam or multi- or single-unit machine, you may select either the preacher curl or the low pulley biceps curl exercise to develop your biceps muscles, and the triceps extension or the press-down exercise to develop your triceps muscles.

How to Perform the Triceps Extension

Assume a sitting position with your back firmly against the pad. Adjust the seat until your shoulders are close to the same height as your elbows. Your elbows should be in line with the axes of the cam. Place your hands, upper arms, and elbows on the appropriate pads. From this position push with your hands until your elbows are completely straight. Do not allow your upper arms to lift off the pads. Pause in the extended position, then slowly return to the starting position. You should exhale when pushing upward through the sticking point and inhale during the return (see Figure 6.5, a-c).

FIGURE
6.5

KEYS TO SUCCESS

TRICEPS EXTENSION
(CAM MACHINE)

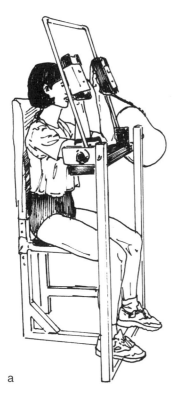

a

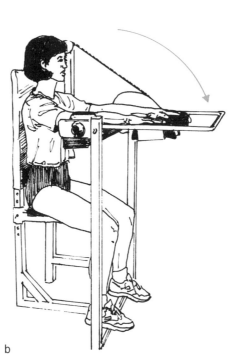

b

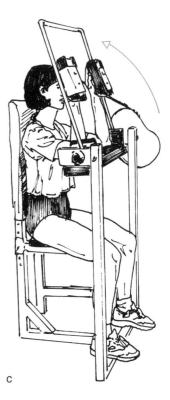

c

Preparation Phase

1. Place back firmly against pad ___
2. Adjust seat so that shoulders are close to the same height as elbows ___
3. Place upper arms and hands on pads ___

Downward Execution Phase

1. Extend elbows completely ___
2. Upper arms stay back, and elbows point forward ___
3. Exhale while passing through sticking point ___

Upward Execution Phase

1. Slowly return to starting position ___
2. Inhale during return to starting position ___

TRICEPS EXTENSION SUCCESS STOPPERS

The errors most common to the triceps extension are associated with acquiring and maintaining the proper body position. Specific examples and suggestions for correcting this and other errors follow.

Error	Correction
1. Your elbows are higher than your shoulders.	1. Adjust the seat to position your elbows more level with your shoulders.
2. Your upper arms and elbows lift off the pads.	2. Keep pressing your upper arms and elbows against the pads—lighten your load if necessary.
3. Your elbows are not in line with the axis of the cam.	3. Adjust the positioning of the upper arms.
4. You do not breathe properly.	4. Exhale when passing through the sticking point, and inhale during the return.

How to Perform the Triceps Press-Down

Assume an erect position facing the weight machine, with your feet approximately shoulder-width apart. Grasp the lat bar in an overhand grip, with your hands no more than 6 inches apart. Begin the exercise with the bar at chest height and upper arms pressed firmly against your ribs.

From this position extend your forearms until your elbows are straight and the bar touches your thighs. Pause, then slowly return the bar to chest height without moving your upper arms and torso. Exhale after passing the sticking point, and inhale during the return (see Figure 6.6, a-c).

FIGURE
6.6

TRICEPS PRESS-DOWN ON LAT BAR
(MULTI- OR SINGLE-UNIT WEIGHT MACHINE)

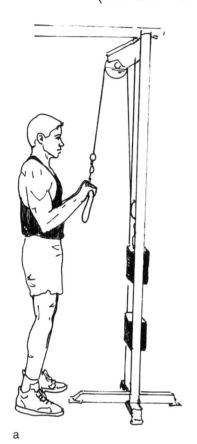

a

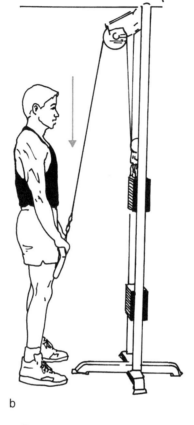

b

c

Preparation Phase

1. Stand erect ___
2. Feet shoulder-width apart ___
3. Overhand grip ___
4. Hands no more than 6 inches apart ___
5. Bar chest-high to begin ___
6. Squeeze upper arms against ribs ___

Downward Execution Phase

1. Extend forearms until bar touches thighs ___
2. Do not move upper arms or torso ___
3. Exhale when passing through sticking point ___
4. Pause ___

Upward Execution Phase

1. Inhale while slowly returning bar to chest height ___
2. Keep wrists straight throughout exercise ___

TRICEPS PRESS-DOWN SUCCESS STOPPERS

The errors most common to the press-down on the lat bar are associated with acquiring and maintaining the proper upper arm position and bar speed.

Specific examples and suggestions for correcting them follow.

Error	Correction
1. Your hands are too far apart.	1. Space your hands no more than 6 inches apart.
2. You allow the bar to move above the shoulders.	2. The bar should begin at chest height and not be allowed to move higher than shoulder level—think, "Knuckles below the shoulders."
3. Your upper arms move away from the side of your ribs during press-down.	3. Squeeze your upper arms against your ribs, and pause at the fully extended and flexed elbow positions.
4. Your elbows are not extended completely.	4. Continue pressing downward until your elbows completely straighten and bar touches thighs.
5. You allow the bar to move rapidly upward to chest height. This causes many of the bar location and arm position errors presented here and imposes an undesirable stress on the elbows, muscles, and joints.	5. Slowly return bar to chest height.
6. Your torso moves back and forth.	6. Maintain a stable, upright position in which your head, shoulders, hips, and feet form a straight line. Lighten the load if necessary.

DEVELOPING THE BICEPS AND TRICEPS

PRACTICE PROCEDURE DRILLS

1. Choose Two Exercises

After reading about the characteristics and techniques involved in the three different exercises and the type of equipment required for each, you are ready to put what you have learned to use. Consider the availability of equipment and your situation, then select two of the following exercises to use in your program.

- Biceps curl and triceps extension (free weight)
- Preacher curl and triceps extension (cam machine)
- Low pulley biceps curl and triceps press-down on lat bar (multi- or single-unit weight machine)

Please turn to Appendix C and copy your two arm exercise choices onto your workout chart.

Success Goal = 2 arm exercises selected ___

Success Check
- Consider availability of equipment ___

2. Determine Trial and Warm-Up Loads

This practice procedure will answer the question, "How much weight or load should I use?" Using the coefficients associated with the arm exercises you selected and the formulas below, determine the trial load. Then round off your results to the nearest 5-pound increment or to the closest weight-stack plate. Use one-half of the amount determined for the trial load for your warm-up load in this exercise.

Trial Load Determination Formula ARM–BICEPS						
Body weight	(Exercise)	×	Coefficient	=	Trial load	Warm-up load
		Female				
BWT = _____	(FW–biceps curl)	×	.23	=	_____	_____
BWT = _____	(C–preacher curl)	×	.12	=	_____	_____
BWT = _____	(M–low pulley biceps curl)	×	.15	=	_____	_____
		Male				
BWT = _____	(FW–biceps curl)	×	.30	=	_____	_____
BWT = _____	(C–preacher curl)	×	.20	=	_____	_____
BWT = _____	(M–low pulley biceps curl)	×	.25	=	_____	_____

BWT = body weight, FW = free weight, C = cam, and M = multi- or single-unit machine exercise.
Note. If you are a male who weighs more than 175 pounds (79.25 kg), then record your body weight as 175 (79.25 kg). If you are a female and weigh over 140 pounds (63.5 kg), then record your body weight as 140 (63.5 kg).

Trial Load Determination Formula ARM–TRICEPS						
Body weight	(Exercise)	×	Coefficient	=	Trial load	Warm-up load
		Female				
BWT = _____	(FW–triceps extension)	×	.12	=	_____	_____
BWT = _____	(C–triceps extension)	×	.13	=	_____	_____
BWT = _____	(M–triceps/press-down on lat bar)	×	.19	=	_____	_____
		Male				
BWT = _____	(FW–triceps extension)	×	.21	=	_____	_____
BWT = _____	(C–triceps extension)	×	.35	=	_____	_____
BWT = _____	(M–triceps/press-down on lat bar)	×	.32	=	_____	_____

BWT = body weight, FW = free weight, C = cam, and M = multi- or single-unit machine exercise.
Note. If you are a male who weighs more than 175 pounds (79.25 kg), then record your body weight as 175 (79.25 kg). If you are a female and weigh over 140 pounds (63.5 kg), then record your body weight as 140 (63.5 kg).

Success Goal = Record both trial and warm-up loads (These loads will be used in the next two drills.) ___

Success Check

• Multiply your body weight by the correct coefficient ___
• Divide trial load by two for the warm-up load ___
• Round off to nearest weight stack for both the training and warm-up loads ___

3. Practice Proper Technique

In this procedure you are to perform 15 reps with the warm-up load determined in practice procedure 2. Focus on the following techniques.

Review the Keys to Success for proper grip and body positioning, and visualize the movement pattern through the full range of motion. When you are ready to execute the exercise, remember to inhale, then use a slow and controlled velocity and exhale through the sticking point. Check your technique either by watching yourself in a mirror or by asking a qualified person to observe and assess your performance in the basic techniques.

Success Goal = 15 reps with calculated warm-up load ___

Success Check

• All reps correctly performed ___

4. Determine Training Load

This practice procedure will help you determine an appropriate training load that is designed to produce from 12 to 15 reps. Use the calculated trial load from practice procedure 2 and perform as many reps as possible with this load.

Success Goal = 12 to 15 reps with calculated trial load ___

Success Check

• Check for correct load ___
• Maintain good technique during each rep ___

If you executed 12 to 15 reps with your trial load, then your trial load becomes your training load. Record this as your "Training load" in Appendix C for this exercise. You are now ready to move on to the next chapter (Step 7).

5. Make Needed Load Adjustments

If you did not complete 12 reps with your trial load, it is too heavy and you should lighten the load. On the other hand, if you performed more than 15 reps, it is too light and you should increase the load. Use the formula and chart below to make necessary adjustments.

Load Adjustment Chart	
Reps completed	Adjustment (in pounds)
<7	−15
8-9	−10
10-11	− 5
16-17	+ 5
18-19	+10
>20	+15

Determining the Training Load Formula				
Trial load (pounds)	+/−	Adjustment	=	Training load (pounds)
_____	+/−	_____	=	_____

Success Goal = Appropriate load adjustments are made ___

Success Check
• Check correct use of Load Adjustment Chart ___
• Record as the "Training load" in Appendix C ___

STEP 7

LEG EXERCISES: SELECTING ONE FOR YOUR PROGRAM

E xercises that develop the upper leg are considered to be very physically demanding, due to the large muscle area involved. The exercises selected are the lunge (free weights) and leg press (machine). These exercises are excellent for the front of the thigh (quadriceps), shown in Appendix B, anterior view, and the back of the thigh (hamstrings) and the hip (gluteals), shown in Appendix B, posterior view. These are multi-joint exercises that involve simultaneously extending the knee and hip joint. The quadriceps extend the knee joint, while the hamstrings flex it and with the help of the gluteals extend the hip joint. The exercises you will be doing contribute to knee and hip joint stabilization, muscle padding for protection of the hip, and lower body "sculpturing." The leg and hip strength gained through them is especially beneficial to those involved in athletic activities.

This area of the body is worked by these exercises sometimes referred to as the "power zone." These muscle groups (quadriceps, hamstrings, and gluteals), the three largest in the body, are responsible for our ability to run, jump, and make quick starts and fast stops, as well as quick lateral, backward, pushing, pulling, rotational, and kicking movements. They also stabilize the upper body while it performs most of its movements. The importance of developing these muscle groups is obvious and must not be neglected in favor of the more visible muscles of the upper body.

Free Weight Exercise

If you have access to free weights, you may select the lunge exercise to develop your legs. If you prefer work-

ing with machines, see the "Machine Exercise" section.

How to Perform the Lunge

The lunge is a relatively difficult exercise to perform because of the balance required. You should try lunges first without weights to develop the needed balance. When you feel comfortable with the forward and backward movements and with your balance, begin using handheld dumbbells. The preparation phase begins with your feet shoulder-width apart, eyes straight ahead, head up, shoulders back, chest out, and back straight. This erect posture should be maintained throughout the exercise (see Figure 7.1a).

The forward execution phase begins with a slow, controlled step forward (Figure 7.1b) on your preferred leg, being careful not to overstride. As shown in Figure 7.1c, your hips are lowered enough so that the top of your (forward) thigh is slightly below parallel and your knee is directly over your ankle. Your front foot should be straight ahead and your back knee relatively extended to stretch your hip flexor muscles. The knee that is back should not quite touch the floor.

The backward execution phase begins by pushing off your front foot and returning to the starting position smoothly without using upper-torso momentum (see Figure 7.1, d-f). Step forward with the other foot in the next rep and continue alternating until the set is completed. At first you might have to slide (stutter step) your foot on the floor in order to return to the starting position. As you gain strength and develop better balance, this will not be necessary.

FIGURE
7.1

KEYS TO SUCCESS

LUNGE
(DUMBBELLS)
Preparation and Forward Execution Phases

a   b   c

1. Overhand grip with arms straight down ___
2. Torso erect, head up, eyes straight forward ___
3. Feet shoulder-width apart ___

4. Upper torso remains erect ___
5. Inhale and push off back foot ___
6. Slow, controlled step forward ___
7. Place front foot straight ahead ___

8. Lower hips until front thigh slightly below parallel ___
9. Keep front knee over ankle ___
10. Back knee extended, but not touching floor ___

Backward Execution Phase

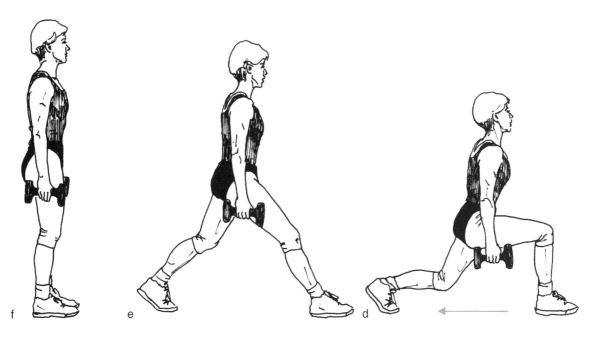

f   e   d

1. Exhale and push off front foot to return to starting position ___
2. Maintain erect torso position ___
3. Keep eyes looking straight ahead ___

LUNGE SUCCESS STOPPERS

Most errors associated with the lunge are the result of stride length and torso movement. You will tend to overstride or understride. It is also common to use upper torso momentum to return to the starting position.

Error	Correction
1. Your front foot is pointed out.	1. Practice stepping on a line, with the thigh, knee, and foot forming a straight line.
2. Your back knee is not extended.	2. Use a mirror to determine needed changes in hip and knee position.
3. Your upper torso leans forward.	3. Keep your head and shoulders up and back and your chest out.

Machine Exercise

If you have access to either a multi- or single-unit machine, you may select the leg press to develop your legs.

How to Perform the Leg Press

This exercise involves the use of either a pulley/pivot or cam-type leg press machine. The preparation phase begins by adjusting the seat so that there is a 90-degree angle or less at the knees. The knees should be apart so that they are not pressed back into the abdomen and chest, which could create difficulty when attempting to inhale. Sit erect, with your lower back against the back of the seat, toes pointed slightly outward, and feet flat against the pedal surface. Grasp the handrails to stabilize your body (see Figure 7.2a).

The forward execution phase (Figure 7.2b) is initiated by pushing your legs to the extended-knee position while maintaining an upright position. The knees should be pressed back toward each other as they are extended. Avoid twisting your body as you extend your legs. Do not "lock out" the knees at any time. Exhale during your press outward, and inhale on your return to the starting position.

The backward execution phase (Figure 7.2c) involves allowing your legs to move back to your body as far as possible without your buttocks lifting up and/or the weight touching the stack. This movement should be performed in a very slow and controlled manner. Allowing the weights to drop quickly back toward the weight stack and stopping them just before they hit could cause injury to your lower back.

FIGURE 7.2 · **KEYS TO SUCCESS**

LEG PRESS
(MULTI- OR SINGLE-UNIT MACHINE)

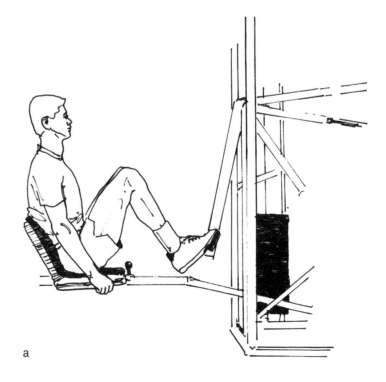

Preparation Phase

1. Torso erect, back against back of seat ___
2. Legs flexed 90 degrees or less ___
3. Feet parallel and flat on pedal surface ___
4. Arms straight, holding handrails ___

a

Forward Execution Phase

1. Push pedals to extended-knee position ___
2. Maintain erect body position ___
3. Do not lock knees ___
4. Avoid twisting body on outward press ___
5. Exhale during outward press ___

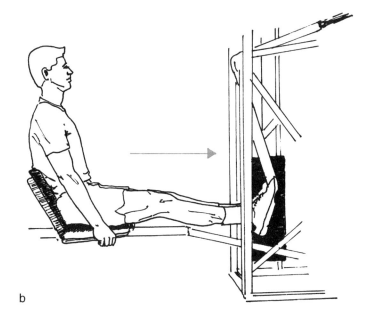

b

Backward Execution Phase

1. Slowly return legs to 90-degree flexion ___
2. Maintain erect body position ___
3. Inhale as the knees are flexing ___

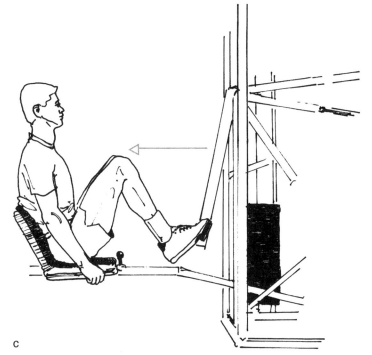

c

LEG PRESS SUCCESS STOPPERS

Most errors associated with the leg press involve the speed of extension and flexion, and locking out the knees. There is a tendency to press out too quickly, causing the knees to lock out. The danger here is that you might hyperextend the knees and cause injury. Another common error is letting the foot pedal weight "free-fall" back to the starting position. Thus, the first step in correcting errors is to slowly extend the knees, then make a slow, controlled movement back to the starting position.

Error	Correction
1. Your feet are not flat on the pedal surface.	1. Think about pushing with the middle or back half of the foot.
2. Your legs are not flexed 90 degrees or less.	2. Use a mirror or ask someone to help you establish a 90-degree angle.
3. Your torso leans forward.	3. Sit with the back and hips pushed against the seat.
4. Your knees are fully locked out at the end of the forward execution phase.	4. Control your forward speed, and concentrate on stopping just before your knees are locked out.

DEVELOPING THE LEGS

PRACTICE PROCEDURE DRILLS

1. Choose One Exercise

After reading about the characteristics and techniques of these two exercises and the type of equipment required for each, you are ready to put what you have learned to use. Consider the availability of equipment in your situation, then select one of the following exercises to use in your program.

- Lunge (free weights)
- Leg press (multi- or single-unit weight machine)

Please turn to Appendix C and copy your leg exercise choice onto your workout chart.

Success Goal = 1 leg exercise selected ___

Success Check
- Consider availability of equipment ___
- Consider time available ___

2. Determine Trial and Warm-Up Loads

This practice procedure answers the question, "How much weight or load should I use?" Using the coefficient associated with the leg exercise you selected and the formula following, determine the trial load. Then round off your results to the closest 5-pound increment or to the closest weight-stack plate. Use one-half of the amount determined for the trial load for your warm-up load in this exercise.

With the Lunge Exercise

Practice without weight until you develop the necessary balance, then begin to add weight by holding handheld dumbbells. Females should add in 10-pound increments (5 pounds in each hand), and males should add in 20-pound increments (10 pounds in each hand). Continue to add weight slowly until you establish a training load that produces 12 to 15 reps.

Trial Load Determination Formula LEGS						
Body weight	(Exercise)	×	Coefficient	=	Trial load	Warm-up load
Female						
BWT = _____	(FW–lunge)	×	.20	=	_____	_____
BWT = _____	(M–leg press)	×	1.0	=	_____	_____
Male						
BWT = _____	(FW–lunge)	×	.20	=	_____	_____
BWT = _____	(M–leg press)	×	1.3	=	_____	_____

BWT = body weight, FW = free weight, C = cam, and M = multi- or single-unit machine exercise.
Note. If you are a male who weighs more than 175 pounds (79.25 kg), then record your body weight as 175 (79.25 kg). If you are a female and weigh over 140 pounds (63.5 kg), then record your body weight as 140 (63.5 kg).

Success Goal = Record both trial and warm-up loads (These loads will be used in the next two procedures.) ___

Success Check
- Multiply your body weight by the correct coefficient ___
- Divide trial load by two for the warm-up load ___
- Round off to nearest weight stack for both the training and warm-up loads ___

3. Practice Proper Technique

In this procedure you are to perform 15 reps with the warm-up load determined in practice procedure 2. Focus on the following techniques.

Review the Keys to Success for proper body positioning, and visualize the movement pattern through the full range of motion. Inhale when you are ready to execute the exercise, then perform the movement with a slow and controlled velocity, remembering to exhale through the sticking point. Ask a qualified person to observe and assess your performance in the basic techniques.

Success Goal = 15 reps with calculated warm-up load ___

Success Check
- All reps correctly performed ___

4. Determine Training Load

This practice procedure will help you determine an appropriate training load that is designed to produce from 12 to 15 reps. If you selected the leg press, use the calculated trial load from practice procedure 2 and perform as many reps as possible with this load. If you selected the lunge exercise, you should gradually increase the weight of the dumbbells until the 12-15 rep range is achieved. Men begin with 10-pound dumbbells and women with 5-pound dumbbells (one in each hand).

Success Goal = 12 to 15 reps with calculated trial load ___

Success Check
• Check for correct load ___
• Maintain good technique during each rep ___

If you executed 12 to 15 reps with your trial load, then your trial load becomes your training load. Record this as your "Training load" in Appendix C for this exercise. You are now ready to move on to the next chapter (Step 8).

5. Make Needed Load Adjustments

If you performed less than 12 reps with your trial load, it is too heavy and you should lighten the load. On the other hand, if you performed more than 15 reps, the load is too light and you should increase it. Use the chart and formula below (described in Step 2) to make necessary adjustments for the leg press. If you selected the lunge exercise, gradually increase the training load until the 12-15 rep range is reached.

Load Adjustment Chart	
Reps completed	Adjustment (in pounds)
<7	−15
8-9	−10
10-11	− 5
16-17	+ 5
18-19	+10
>20	+15

Determining the Training Load Formula				
Trial load (pounds)	+/−	Adjustment	=	Training load (pounds)
_____	+/−	_____	=	_____

Success Goal = Appropriate load adjustments are made ___

Success Check
• Check correct use of Load Adjustment Chart ___
• Record as the "Training load" in Appendix C ___

STEP 8

ABDOMEN EXERCISES: SELECTING ONE FOR YOUR PROGRAM

The abdominal muscles are the major supporting muscles for the stomach area. They not only support and protect internal organs, but also aid the muscles of the lower back to align and support the spine for good posture and lifting activities. Properly developed abdominal muscles serve as a biological girdle to flatten your waistline. Although there is no such thing as spot reducing (fat reduction in only one area), strong abdominal muscles make the area smaller and look tighter even though the fat may still be there. The abdominal muscles (shown in Appendix B, anterior view) include the rectus abdominis, which causes the trunk to bend or flex forward, and the external obliques, which assist the rectus abdominis and cause trunk rotation and bending to the side.

The exercises described here will be the twisting trunk curl and the machine abdominal curl. These exercises should be performed on a regular basis, three to five times each week. The straight-leg (knees straight) sit-up is not included here because it relies heavily on hip flexors (rectus femoris and iliopsoas) and does not emphasize working the abdominal muscles; it may also contribute to lower back problems.

No-Weight Exercise

You may select the twisting trunk curl exercise to develop your abdominal muscles. Or, if you prefer working with machines, see the "Machine Exercise" section.

How to Perform the Twisting Trunk Curl

Prepare for this exercise by lying with your back on the floor and your feet on a bench or chair. Fold your arms across your chest, with your hands on opposite shoulders.

The upward execution begins as you inhale, pull your chin to your chest, and then contract the abdominal muscles to move your torso upward. Alternately curl your shoulders toward the opposite knee and exhale when nearing the point of greatest flexion (upward position). This movement should be slow and controlled without using momentum by lunging forward with the head, arms, and shoulders. Pause briefly at this point.

The downward execution follows the pause at the top. Begin to inhale at this point. Be sure to keep your chin on your chest until your shoulders touch the floor (see Figure 8.1, a-c). Then allow your head to touch. This part of the exercise should also be slow and controlled (by keeping your abdominals contracted) so that you receive equal benefit from both the upward and downward phase. Your lower back and hips should remain in contact with the floor throughout the exercise. A high number of reps is encouraged to promote tone, muscular endurance, strength, and muscle definition. However, you should not sacrifice quality for quantity. If you practice correct techniques, the numbers will gradually improve over time and reward you with the desired results.

After you have performed this exercise successfully for a period of time and find that it has become too easy, you might want to increase difficulty the following ways: (1) Place your hands behind your head or lightly touch your ears to give the added weight of your arms. Be sure that you never pull upward on your head, as this could cause soreness or injury to your neck muscles. (2) Use an incline board but keep in mind that as the resistance increases it becomes more and more important to adhere strictly to the correct techniques mentioned previously. The degree of incline of the board increases the resistance of your upper body; therefore, the greater the incline, the greater the resistance. Use this board cautiously and don't try to increase the angle of incline too rapidly.

FIGURE
8.1

KEYS TO SUCCESS

TWISTING TRUNK CURL

Preparation Phase

1. Back flat on floor ___
2. Feet on bench or chair ___
3. Arms folded across chest ___
4. Inhale ___

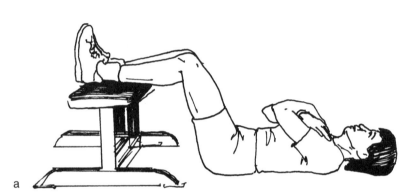

a

Upward Execution Phase

1. Chin to chest first ___
2. Alternately curl shoulders and upper back toward opposite knee ___
3. Exhale when nearing highest position ___
4. Pause momentarily ___

b

Downward Execution Phase

1. Return slowly to starting position ___
2. Keep chin to chest until shoulders touch ___
3. Inhale during downward movement ___

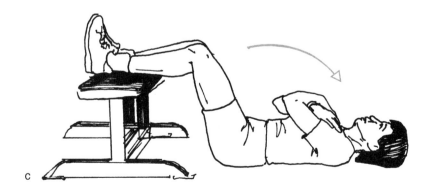

c

TWISTING TRUNK CURL SUCCESS STOPPERS

Most errors associated with the twisting trunk curl involve speed of movement. You will have a tendency to lunge forward and then quickly fall back to the starting position. Keep the movements slow and controlled in both the upward and the downward movement phases.

Error	Correction
1. Your buttocks lift off the floor just prior to upward movement.	1. Start the exercise with your head, shoulders, upper back, and lower back in contact with the floor. Keep your lower back and buttocks in contact with the floor throughout each rep.
2. Your chin is not on your chest.	2. Curl your chin to your chest to begin the upward movement.
3. You use momentum to complete the movement.	3. Concentrate on using your abdominals only to complete the movement.
4. Your shoulders lower rapidly, followed by bouncing action upward.	4. Slowly lower your upper back, shoulders, and head to the starting position. Pause on the floor before beginning another rep.

Machine Exercise

If you have access to a cam machine, you may select the trunk curl exercise to develop your abdominal muscles.

How to Perform the Trunk Curl

Assume an erect sitting position, with your shoulders and upper arms firmly against the pads. Adjust the height of the seat so that the axis of rotation is level with the lower part of your sternum (midchest). Place your ankles behind the roller pad, with your knees spread and your hands crossing in front of you (see Figure 8.2a). While maintaining this position, shorten the distance between your rib cage and navel by contracting your abdominals only (see Figure 8.2b). Pause in the fully contracted position, then return slowly to the starting position (see Figure 8.2c). Exhale during contraction, and inhale during relaxation. You may encounter some cam machines that have a roller in front of your stomach to grasp.

FIGURE 8.2

KEYS TO SUCCESS

TRUNK CURL
(CAM MACHINE)

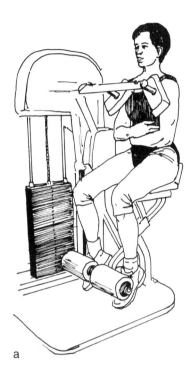

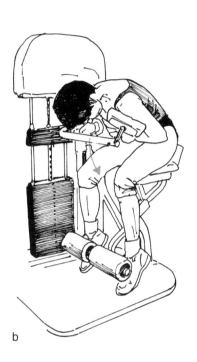

a

b

c

Preparation Phase

1. Sit with shoulders and upper arms firmly against the pads ___
2. Adjust seat so axis of rotation is level with lower part of sternum ___
3. Place ankles behind roller pads ___
4. Spread knees and sit erect ___
5. Cross arms ___

Downward Execution Phase

1. Shorten distance between rib cage and navel by contracting abdominals only ___
2. Keep legs relaxed as chest is lowered ___
3. Exhale during contraction ___
4. Pause in contracted position ___

Upward Execution Phase

1. Return slowly to starting position ___
2. Inhale while returning to the starting position ___

TRUNK CURL SUCCESS STOPPERS

The errors commonly observed in the trunk curl exercise concern body positioning and using the hands and shoulders instead of relying solely on the abdominal muscles to bring the upper body forward. Specific examples of these errors and how to correct them are presented next.

Error	Correction
1. Your shoulders and upper arms come off the pads.	1. Think, "Shoulders and upper arms firmly against the pads throughout the exercise."
2. Your axis of rotation is not level with the lower part of your sternum.	2. Adjust the seat so your axis of rotation is level with the lower part of your sternum.
3. You pull with your hands and shoulders.	3. Concentrate on contracting your abdominals only.

DEVELOPING THE ABDOMINALS

PRACTICE PROCEDURE DRILLS

1. Choose One Exercise

After reading about the characteristics and techniques of the two different exercises and the type of equipment required for each, you are ready to put what you have learned to use. Consider what equipment is available to you, then select one of the following exercises to use in your program.

- Twisting trunk curl (no weight)
- Trunk curl (cam machine)

Please turn to Appendix C and record your choice.

Success Goal = 1 abdominal exercise selected ___

Success Check
- Consider availability of equipment ___
- Consider time available ___

2. Determine Trial and Warm-Up Loads

This practice procedure will answer the question, "How much weight or load should I use?" For the trunk curl (cam machine) exercise, use the formula below.

If you chose the twisting trunk curl, you will not need to establish warm-up, trial, and training loads. Continue on with the following practice procedures and ignore comments concerning warm-up and training loads. If you chose the machine trunk curl, follow the procedures as they are described.

Trial Load Determination Formula ABDOMINALS						
Body weight	(Exercise)	×	Coefficient	=	Trial load	Warm-up load
Female						
BWT = _____	(twisting trunk curl)	×		=	no load _____	no load _____
BWT = _____	(C–trunk curl)	×	.20	=	_____	_____
Male						
BWT = _____	(twisting trunk curl)	×		=	no load _____	no load _____
BWT = _____	(C–trunk curl)	×	.20	=	_____	_____

BWT = body weight, and C = cam.
Note. If you are a male who weighs more than 175 pounds (79.25 kg), then record your body weight as 175 (79.25 kg). If you are a female and weigh over 140 pounds (63.5 kg), then record your body weight as 140 (63.5 kg).

Success Goal = Record both trial and warm-up loads (These loads will be used in the next two procedures.) ___

Success Check
- Multiply your body weight by the correct coefficient ___
- Divide trial load by two for the warm-up load ___
- Round off to nearest weight stack for both the training and warm-up loads ___

3. Practice Proper Technique

In this procedure you are to perform 15 reps with the warm-up load determined in practice procedure 2. Focus on the following techniques.

Review the Keys to Success for proper body positioning, and visualize the movement pattern through the full range of motion. Inhale when you are ready to execute the exercise, then perform the movement with a slow and controlled velocity, remembering to exhale through the sticking point. Ask a qualified person to observe and assess your performance in the basic techniques.

Success Goal = 15 reps with calculated warm-up load ___

Success Check
- All reps correctly performed ___

4. Determine Training Load

This practice procedure will help you determine an appropriate training load designed to produce from 12 to 15 reps. Use the calculated trial load from practice procedure 2 and perform as many reps as possible with this load. If you selected the twisting trunk curl, no calculation is needed. Simply perform as many twisting trunk curls as possible.

Success Goal = 12 to 15 reps with calculated trial load ___

Success Check
• Check for correct load ___
• Maintain good technique during each rep ___

If you executed 12 to 15 reps with your trial load, then your trial load becomes your training load. Record this as your "Training load" in Appendix C for this exercise. You are now ready to move on to the next chapter (Step 9).

5. Make Needed Load Adjustments

If you performed less than 12 reps with your trial load, it is too heavy and you should lighten the load. On the other hand, if you performed more than 15 reps, the load is too light and you should increase it. Use the chart and formula below as described in Step 2 (Figure 2.3) to make necessary adjustments for the trunk curl.

Load Adjustment Chart	
Reps completed	Adjustment (in pounds)
<7	−15
8-9	−10
10-11	− 5
16-17	+ 5
18-19	+10
>20	+15

Determining the Training Load Formula				
Trial load (pounds)	+/−	Adjustment	=	Training load (pounds)
_____	+/−	_____	=	_____

Success Goal = Appropriate load adjustments are made ___

Success Check
• Check correct use of Load Adjustment Chart ___
• Record as the "Training load" in Appendix C ___

STEP 9

THE BASIC PROGRAM: CHARTING YOUR WORKOUTS

N ow the fun really begins, because this is when you start training! This step takes you through a series of tasks necessary to complete your first workout and to make needed changes in the workouts that follow it. Each workout should contain three parts: a proper warm-up, one exercise for each of the large muscle groups (as you select in Steps 3-8), and a proper cool-down.

The basic program is well-balanced and gets you started on a training schedule. You don't have to worry about what exercises to include, in what order to do them, how many reps to do, how many sets to do, or when to make load changes—these decisions have already been made for you. You will need to follow this basic program for at least 6 weeks before tailoring it in any way. This program is designed to slowly improve your muscular endurance and give your body time to adapt to the new demands being placed on it.

Why Follow the Basic Program?

For maximum benefits, make a commitment to training three times a week, and allow yourself a day of rest between workouts; e.g., work out on M-W-F or T-Th-Sat. If you can only train twice a week, allow no more than 3 days between training sessions; e.g., M-Th, T-Sat, or W-Sat. With consistency you will notice that as your muscular endurance improves in response to training, your ability to recover from the fatigue of each set will also improve.

The basic program builds in 12 to 15 repetitions per exercise, with one set during the first workout, two sets during workouts #2 through #4, and three sets during workouts #5 through #18. The first four workouts provide sufficient stress to prepare your body for the more strenuous workouts (#5 through #18).

The recovery time between each set is 1 minute until workout #5, at which time you might consider shortening the rest periods from 1 minute to 45 or 30 seconds. Rest periods shorter that 30 seconds do not provide sufficient time to recover. The advantage of shortening the rest periods is that you reduce the amount of time needed to complete a training session. It will also help to improve your level of muscular endurance. The disadvantage is that if you do not give yourself adequate rest, the number of reps completed will be fewer. This means you are not accomplishing what you set out to do (i.e., perform more reps in each exercise). Pay attention to the length of the rest periods, and try to be consistent between sets and workouts. Give yourself time to fully recover between sets.

When you are able to perform 2 or more reps above the intended number (i.e., 17 or more) in the last set on 2 consecutive training days (the 2-for-2 rule), it is time to increase the load. Or, if you are unable to perform 12 reps in two consecutive training sessions, it is time to decrease the load. Refer to the Load Adjustment Chart in practice procedure 5 in Step 2, and make appropriate changes in the training load. Keep in mind two very important points while training. First, all reps should be performed with excellent technique—do not sacrifice technique for additional reps. The quality (technique used) in performing each rep is more important than the number performed. Give each rep in each set your best effort, and apply the 2-for-2 rule to keep the number of reps between 12 and 15 in each set.

CHARTING YOUR WORKOUTS WITHIN THE BASIC PROGRAM DRILLS

Note: Make three copies of the Workout Chart in Appendix C in order to record your basic program results for 6 weeks. Remember to properly warm up before each workout and properly cool down afterward (review guidelines in Step 2). Use the following drills to determine when and how to make needed changes in your workouts.

1. Workout #1

For your first workout, perform 1 set of each of the exercises in the order listed on your Workout Chart in Appendix C. If the training loads are correct, you should be able to perform 12 to 15 repetitions in each set; if not, make adjustments as described in practice procedure 5 in Step 2.

After completing a set of an exercise, rest approximately 1 minute before starting the next exercise. On your Workout Chart, record reps in each set under the proper heading, i.e. for Day 1. Figure 9.1 illustrates where to write in loads and reps performed.

Weight Training Workout Chart (3-Days-a-Week)

Name: _Tom Brown_   Workout day # ____   Week # ____

Order	Muscle area	Exercise	Training load	Set	Day 1 — 1	2	3	Day 2 — 1	2	3	Day 3 — 1	2	3
1	Chest	Bench press	90	Wt.	90								
				Reps	13								
2	Back	Bent over row	80	Wt.	80								
				Reps	12								
3	Shoulder	Standing press	60	Wt.	60								
				Reps	15								
4	Arms (front of)	Biceps curl	75	Wt.	75								
				Reps	15								
5	Arms (back of)	Triceps press-down	30	Wt.	30								
				Reps	12								
6	Legs	Leg press	165	Wt.	165								
				Reps	15								
7	Abdomen	Trunk curl	—	Wt.	—								
				Reps	20								

Annotations: Set #1 | Load goes here | Number of reps goes here

Figure 9.1 Recording loads and reps.

Success Goal = 1 set of each exercise is performed and recorded on workout chart ___

Success Check
- Check to see that load selection is correct and bars are loaded evenly ___
- Secure plates and bars, and selection key in weight stacks ___
- Use proper exercise and spotting (with free weights) techniques ___
- Make appropriate load adjustments ___

2. Workouts #2 Through #4

If you are training with a partner, arrange your workouts so that you alternate turns performing an exercise until both of you have completed the desired number of sets. Perform two sets of each of the exercises in the order listed on your Workout Chart in Appendix C. Again, if the training loads are correct, you should be able to perform 12 to 15 reps within a set; if not, you will need to make adjustments as described in practice procedure 5 in Step 2. After completing a set of an exercise, rest one minute before starting the next set. On your Workout Chart, record reps and sets completed under the proper headings, i.e., for Day 2, Day 3, Day 4. See figure 9.2 for an example of how to record your reps and sets for workouts #2 through #4, and for workouts #5 through #18 (see next drill).

Weight Training Workout Chart (3-Days-a-Week Program)

Name: Tom Brown

Order	Muscle area	Exercise	Training load	Set	Week # — Day 1 1	Day 1 2	Day 1 3	Day 2 1	Day 2 2	Day 2 3	Day 3 1	Day 3 2	Day 3 3	Week # — Day 1 1	Day 1 2	Day 1 3	Day 2 1	Day 2 2	Day 2 3
1	Chest	Bench press	90	Wt.	90			90	90		90	90		90	90		90	90	90
				Reps	13			12	12		14	12		15	14		16	15	12
2	Back	Bent over row	80	Wt.	80			80	80		80	80		80	80		80	80	80
				Reps	12			13	12		14	13		14	14		15	14	12
3	Shoulder	Standing press	60	Wt.	60			60	60		60	60		60	60		65	65	65
				Reps	15			15	13		16	15		17	17		15	12	12
4	Arms (front of)	Bicep curl	75	Wt.	75			75	75		75	75		75	75		75	75	75
				Reps	15			14	14		15	14		16	15		17	16	15
5	Arms (back of)	Tricep press down	30	Wt.	30			30	30		30	30		30	30		30	30	30
				Reps	12			12	11		14	12		15	15		17	15	13
6	Legs	Leg press	165	Wt.	165			165	165		170	170		170	170		170	170	170
				Reps	15			17	17		14	13		16	15		18	16	15
7	Abdomen	Trunk curl	—	Wt.	—														
				Reps	20			25	20		25	23		30	25		30	30	25
8				Wt.															
				Reps															
9				Wt.							2 sets						start		
				Reps							in workouts						3 sets		
10				Wt.							#2,3,4						in workout		
				Reps													#5 and		
11				Wt.													continues through		
				Reps													workout #18		
12				Wt.															
				Reps															
	Body weight				140			141			140			142			141		
	Date				9/23			9/25			9/27			9/30			10/2		
	Comments				one set first workout, 2 sets in workouts 2,3,4									3 sets starting in workout 5					

Figure 9.2 Sample record of workouts #2 through #4 followed by workouts #5 through #18.

Success Goal = 2 sets of each exercise in basic program performed and recorded on Workout Chart ___

Success Check
• Monitor your rest periods between exercises and workouts ___
• Use good exercise and spotting techniques ___

3. Workouts #5 Through #18

Starting in workout #5, perform 3 (instead of 2) sets of each exercise. The challenge again is to keep the loads heavy or light enough so that you are performing 12-15 reps with excellent technique! Ask your training partner to use the Keys to Success items (within Steps 3 through 8) as a checklist for evaluating the technique used for your selected exercises. Use this feedback to improve your technique. Be especially concerned with breathing and controlling the speed of movement throughout the range of each exercise. Consider shortening rest periods to 45 or 30 seconds.

Record all 3 sets on your Workout Chart (review Figure 9.2). Use the summary guidelines in Table 9.1 for when to make needed changes.

Table 9.1 Making Workout Changes Summary		
Variable	Workouts #2-#4	Workouts #5-#18
Reps	12 to 15	12 to 15
Sets	2 sets	3 sets
Rest-period	1 minute	30 seconds to 1 minute
Loads	Continue to make changes in the loads so that they are heavy/light enough to produce 12 to 15 reps	

Success Goal = 3 sets of each exercise in basic program performed and recorded on the Workout Chart ___

Success Check

• Quality (technique used) of the reps is more important that the number of reps ___
• Apply the 2-for-2 rule (to keep reps between 12 and 15 in each set) ___

LOOKING AHEAD

When workout #18 has been completed (in 6 weeks in a 3-days-a-week program), you should begin a new training approach. In preparation for this, you should now begin to read and complete the tasks described in Steps 10, 11, and 12. These steps describe ways to modify your current program so that it meets your specific needs and interests, and provides ways to stimulate continued improvement.

STEP 10

PROGRAM DESIGN CONSIDERATIONS: MANIPULATING TRAINING VARIABLES

I n this step you will be helped to better understand the "whys and hows" of well-conceived weight training programs. The elements of exercise selection, exercise arrangement, loads, reps, sets, recovery period, and training frequency, referred to as *program design variables*, are the central variables of well-conceived programs. These seven program design variables are grouped into the following three sections, each of which will be discussed.

1. Selecting and Arranging Exercises
2. Determining Training
   - Loads
   - Reps and Sets
   - Rest Period Length
3. Deciding Training Frequency

Why Is It Important to Learn About Program Design Concepts?

Just as certain ingredients in your favorite dish must be included in proper amounts and at the correct time, so too must the sets, reps, and loads in your workouts. The workout "recipe," referred to as *program design*, is what (along with your commitment to training) ultimately determines the success of your weight training program. The exciting thing about developing a knowledge concerning exercise selection and arrangement, loads to use, reps and sets to perform, and training frequency is that you can then design your own programs.

Selecting and Arranging Exercises

The exercises you select will determine which of your muscles become stronger, more enduring, and thicker, and their arrangement will affect the intensity of your workouts. The following discussion is designed to help you better understand issues associated with exercise selection, and is followed by one that explains how to arrange the exercises you select.

Selecting Exercises

An advanced program may include as many as 20 exercises. However, a beginning or basic program (which is what you are following) need only include one exercise for each of the large muscle areas. Muscle areas of particular importance here are the chest (pectoralis major and minor), arms—biceps (biceps brachii and brachialis) and triceps, shoulders (deltoid), back (latissimus dorsi, trapezius, rhomboids), thighs (quadriceps and hamstrings), and abdomen (rectus abdominis and internal and external obliques).

In Steps 3 through 8 you selected one exercise for each of these muscle areas. You are now encouraged to consider adding exercises for the forearm, lower back, and calves because doing so will give you a more rounded program that includes exercises for the major, and most of the "minor," muscle groups. If you are training to improve your athletic performance, you should seriously consider adding one or more of the total body exercises described in Appendix A. Such exercises involve several large muscle groups, making them more physically demanding than those in the basic program. Athletes in wrestling and football should also add one or more exercises for the neck.

Now is the time to also consider adding exercises for a particular muscle area that you believe is especially weak or for areas in which you would like additional muscle tone or size. Appendix A, "Alternative Exercises," includes exercises that will assist you in doing this. You might also consider exchanging one exercise for another that you believe is more enjoyable or more effective. Appendix A, which includes exercises categorized by the muscle area they work, and Appendix B ("Muscles of the Body"), which will help you recognize the names and locations of particular muscles and muscle areas, will assist you in your selection process. Before making a final decision on which exercises to select, you should acquire an understanding of the concepts and principles that are presented next.

Apply the Specificity Concept

Your task is to determine the muscle groups from Appendix B that you really want to develop, then determine which exercises will recruit those muscles. This involves application of a very important concept, the *specificity concept*. This concept refers to training in a specific manner to produce outcomes that are specific to that method of training. For example, developing the chest requires exercises that recruit chest muscles, whereas developing the thigh requires exercises that recruit thigh muscles.

Even the specific angle at which a muscle is called into action determines whether and to what extent a muscle or muscles will be stimulated. For example, Figure 10.1 illustrates how a change in body position changes the specific angle at which the barbell is lowered and pushed upward from the chest. The angle at which the bar is pushed dictates whether the shoulder muscles or the middle or lower portion of the chest muscles become more or less involved in the exercise.

The type and width of the grip are equally impor-

tant, because they also change the angle at which muscles become involved and thus influence the effect on the muscles. For example, a wide grip in the bench press results in greater chest development than a narrow grip. That's why it is so important to perform exercises exactly as they are described in this text.

Consider the Need for Balance

Select "pairs" of exercises to help balance the strength and size of opposing muscle groups. The former is important for creating strong joints, and the latter for developing a proportional physique and good posture.

Pair up opposing muscle group exercises like this:

- Chest with upper back
- Front of upper arm with back of upper arm
- Front (palm side) of forearm with back (knuckle side) of forearm
- Abdominal with lower back
- Front of thigh with back of thigh
- Front of lower leg with back of lower leg

Consider Equipment Needs

Consider what equipment is needed. Determine the equipment needs for each exercise before making a final decision. You may not have the necessary equipment.

Consider the Need for a Spotter

Determine whether a spotter is needed in the exercises you are considering. If one is needed and there is not a qualified spotter available, choose a different exercise to work the same muscle group.

Consider the Time Required

Be aware that the more exercises you decide to include in your program, the longer your workouts will take. It is a common mistake to include too many! Plan for approximately 2 minutes per exercise set, unless you plan to pursue a program specifically designed to develop strength. If strength is your goal, you'll need to plan on about 4 minutes per exercise set. Also, do not forget to consider the number of sets in determining the total workout time re-

a Incline position
Shoulders become more involved

b Horizontal position
Middle section of chest becomes more involved

c Decline position
Lower section of chest becomes more involved

d

Figure 10.1   Effect of changing body position to alter muscle involvement. Changes in body position affect the angle at which the barbell is lowered and raised from the chest (a-c), thus influencing muscle involvement (d).

quired. This is discussed in greater detail later in this step.

Exercise Arrangement

There are many ways to arrange exercises in a workout. The order of exercises affects the intensity of training and is, therefore, a very important consideration. For instance, alternating upper and lower body exercises does not produce as high an intensity level as performing all lower body exercises first. Exercises that involve multiple joints and muscles (referred to as multi-joint exercises) are more intense than those that involve only one joint and less muscle (referred to as single-joint exercises).

The following list presents the two most common arrangements.

- Exercise large muscle groups before small muscles
- Alternate push with pull exercises

Exercise Large Muscle Groups First (L/S)

Exercising the large (L) muscle groups before smaller (S) groups is an approach that is accepted by many. For example, rather than exercising the calf (a smaller muscle group), then exercising the thigh (a larger muscle group), thigh exercises would be performed first. Note that although the muscle area of the upper arms is considered a large muscle area, the front and back are viewed individually and are referred to as small muscle groups. An example of the method of arranging exercises with the large muscle group first is shown in Table 10.1.

Table 10.1 Exercise Arrangement: Large Muscle Groups First		
Exercise	Type (L/S)	Muscle group
Lunge	Large	Thigh and hip
Heel raises	Small	Calf
Bench press	Large	Chest
Triceps extension	Small	Arm (posterior)
Lat pull-down	Large	Upper back
Biceps curl	Small	Arm (anterior)

Alternate Push With Pull Exercises (PS/PL)

You may also arrange exercises so that those resulting in extension of joints are alternated with those that flex joints. Extension exercises require that you "push," whereas flexion exercises require you to "pull"—thus the name of this arrangement, push (PS) with pull (PL). An example would be the triceps extension (push), followed by the biceps curl (pull). This is a good arrangement to use because the same muscle is not worked back to back; that is, the same muscle group is not worked two or more times in succession. This arrangement should give your

muscles sufficient time to recover. An example of this method of arranging exercises is shown in Table 10.2.

Table 10.2 Exercise Arrangement: Alternate Push With Pull		
Exercise	Type (PS/PL)	Muscle group
Bench press	Push	Chest
Lat pull-down	Pull	Back
Seated press	Push	Shoulder
Biceps curl	Pull	Arm (anterior)
Triceps extension	Push	Arm (posterior)
Leg curl	Pull	Thigh (posterior)
Knee extension	Push	Thigh (anterior)

Additional Arrangement Considerations

Two other exercise arrangement issues need to be considered, both of which affect the intensity of your workout.

Sets Performed in Succession Versus Alternating Sets

When more than one set of an exercise is going to be performed, you need to decide whether you will perform all sets of an exercise one after another (in succession) or alternate them with other exercises. Arrangements of exercises performed for 3 sets in succession and alternated are shown below:

In succession = **shoulder press, shoulder press, shoulder press**

Alternated = **shoulder press,** biceps curl, **shoulder press,** lunge, **shoulder press,** trunk curl

Alternated = **shoulder press,** biceps curl, lunge, sit-ups (repeated three times)

In each of these arrangements, 3 sets of shoulder presses are performed, each with an intervening rest period. The "in succession" arrangement is the approach preferred by most.

Triceps and Biceps Exercises After Other Upper Body Exercises

When arranging exercises in your program, be sure that triceps extensions, triceps push-downs, and other elbow extension exercises are *not* performed before pushing exercises such as the bench/chest press or standing/seated press. These pushing exercises rely on assistance from elbow extension strength from the triceps muscles. When triceps exercises precede pushing exercises, they fatigue the triceps, reducing the number of reps and the desired effect on the chest and shoulder muscles, respectively. The same logic applies to biceps exercises. Pulling exercises that involve flexion of the elbow, such as the lat pull-down, are dependent upon strength from biceps muscles. Performing biceps curls before the lat pull-down exercise will fatigue these muscles, reducing the number of lat pull-down reps and the exercise's desired effect on the back muscles.

SELECTING AND ARRANGING EXERCISES

DRILLS

1. Specificity Concept Self-Assessment Quiz

This drill requires reviewing the exercises in Steps 3 through 8 and in Appendix A. Demonstrate your understanding of the specificity concept by marking in the left-hand column a *C* (correct) where an exercise and the primary muscle area developed are correctly aligned, and an *I* (for incorrect) where they are not. Can you find the four that are incorrect?

Specificity Concept Self-Assessment Quiz

Exercise	*Primary muscle area developed*
__ 1. Back extension	Lower back
__ 2. Supine triceps extension	Back of upper arm
__ 3. Standing press	Back
__ 4. Heel raises	Calf
__ 5. Lunge	Thighs and hips
__ 6. Bent over row	Upper back
__ 7. Trunk curl	Abdomen
__ 8. Shoulder shrug	Shoulders
__ 9. Upright row	Chest
__ 10. Concentration curl	Front of upper arm
__ 11. Wrist flexion	Palm side of forearm
__ 12. Lat pull-down	Lower back
__ 13. Bent-leg deadlift	Lower back
__ 14. Hang clean	Forearms
__ 15. Back squat	Thigh and hips

Success Goal = Locate and correct the 4 incorrect matches between the exercise and the muscle developed ___

Success Check
• Apply your knowledge of the muscle locations in Appendix B ___
• Apply knowledge of exercises in Steps 3-8 and in Appendix A ___

Self-Assessment Quiz Answers

The four incorrect matches are listed below.

1. **3 (should be shoulders)**
2. **9 (should be shoulders)**
3. **12 (should be upper back)**
4. **14 (total body exercise; refer to Appendix A)**

2. Balanced (Paired) Exercises Self-Assessment Quiz

Identify the two correctly and incorrectly paired exercises in the following quiz. Use the letter *C* to identify those that are correct, use an *I* for those that are incorrect, then correct the incorrect pairs.

Paired Exercises Self-Assessment Quiz

a. ___ Back extensions—bent-leg deadlift
b. ___ Knee flexion—knee extension
c. ___ Concentration curl—triceps extension
d. ___ Dumbbell fly—bent-knee sit-ups

Success Goal = 4 pairs of exercises are appropriately marked ___

Success Check
• Apply knowledge of muscle balance in all 4 examples ___

Self-Assessment Quiz Answers

The two correct and incorrect pairs of exercises follow:

1. **a (should be back extensions matched with bent-knee sit-ups, trunk curl, or twisting trunk curl exercises)**
2. **b is correct**
3. **c is correct**
4. **d (should be dumbbell fly matched with bent over row, lat pull-down, or rowing exercises)**

3. Arranging Exercises Self-Assessment Quiz

Before you are able to fully understand how to arrange exercises in a workout, you need to be able to recognize the characteristics displayed by them. Consider the size of the muscles, the push-pull movement patterns, and the body parts involved in each of the following exercises. Then fill in the missing quiz information using the letters *L* (large muscle exercise) or *S* (small muscle exercise), and *PS* (pushing exercises) or *PL* (pulling exercises).

Recognizing Exercise Characteristics Self-Assessment Quiz

Exercise	*Type of exercise*	
	L/S	*PS/PL*
1. Dumbbell fly	____	____
2. Wrist flexion	____	____
3. Supine triceps press	____	____
4. Back squat	____	____
5. Trunk curl	____	____
6. Biceps curl	____	____
7. Concentration curl	____	____
8. Heel raise	____	____
9. Upright row	____	____
10. Knee extension	____	____

Success Goal = 20 exercise characteristics are properly identified as follows:
a. 10 types of exercises under the L/S column ___
b. 10 types of exercises under the PS/PL column ___

Success Check
• Apply knowledge of muscle size ___
• Apply knowledge of push-pull exercise character-istics ___

Self-Assessment Quiz Answers

The correct exercise characteristics follow:

Exercise	*Type of exercise*	
	L/S	*PS/PL*
1. Dumbbell fly	L	PL
2. Wrist flexion	S	PL
3. Supine triceps press	S	PS
4. Back squat	L	PS
5. Trunk curl	L	PL
6. Biceps curl	S	PL
7. Concentration curl	S	PL
8. Heel raise	S	PS
9. Upright row	L	PL
10. Knee extension	L	PS

Determining Training Loads, Reps, and Sets

Now that you have a better understanding of exercise selection and arrangement, the next step in designing your own program is to decide on the loads to use. There are many differing opinions concerning this program design variable; however, there is general consensus that decisions should be based on the specificity concept and what is referred to as the *overload principle*. The overload principle asserts that each workout should place a demand on the muscle or muscles that is greater than in the previous workout. Training that incorporates this principle challenges the body to meet and adapt to greater than normal physiological stress. As it does, a new threshold is established that requires an even greater stress to produce an overload. Introducing overloads in a systematic manner is sometimes referred to as *progressive overload*.

Methods for Determining Loads

Determining the load to use is one of the most confusing, yet probably *the* most important, aspect of designing a program. It is important because the load selected determines the number of repetitions you will be able to perform and the amount of rest you need between sets and exercises. It also influences your decisions concerning the number of sets and the frequency at which you should train. Two approaches that can be taken when deciding on the amount of load to use in training are described next.

12-15RM Method

In Steps 3 through 8 your body weight was used to determine initial training loads. The calculations were designed to produce light loads so that you could concentrate on developing correct technique and avoid undue stress on bones and joint structures. Your goal was to identify a load that resulted in 12 to 15 reps. This method of determining a load that will produce muscular failure at 12 to 15 reps is referred to as a 12-15RM method for assigning loads. The letter *R* is an abbreviation for "repetition" and the *M*

is for "maximum," meaning the maximum amount of load that you succeeded with for 12 to 15 reps.

1RM Method

Another method that could have been used is the 1RM method—a single (1) repetition (R) maximum (M) effort. Or said another way, this is the maximum amount of load that you can succeed with for 1 repetition in an exercise. Although this is not a perfect method to use, it is more accurate than using body weight, especially when you have developed good exercise techniques and are conditioned to safely handle heavier loads. This is not an appropriate method for a beginner, however, because it requires greater skill and a level of conditioning developed only through training. Furthermore, this method is not appropriate for all exercises.

This method of determining loads should be used only with exercises that involve more than one joint and recruit large muscle groups that can withstand heavy training loads. Exercises with these characteristics are sometimes referred to as *core* exercises. The term "core" also indicates that these exercises are focal points of your training (that is, you are building the program around them). Examples of core exercises in your workout include those presented for the chest and shoulders (Steps 3 and 5) and the squat and power clean (total body exercises) in Appendix A.

Soon you will be instructed to determine the 1RM for several core exercises. But first, realize that you should keep the number of sets to 3 and the number of reps at 12 to 15 in other exercises. Gradually increase the number of reps to 15 to 30 per set in the abdominal exercises (performed without weights). The rationale for the greater number of reps suggested here for the abdominal exercises is that you are using a light load (your upper body weight), which should make it easier to perform a greater number.

Caution: Before undertaking an effort to predict a 1RM, be sure you have perfected your exercise technique and have at least 5 weeks of training "under your belt."

Procedures for Predicting the 1RM

To provide you with experience at using the 1RM method, you are given eight procedures for determining the 1RM with the chest exercise you selected in Step 3. Fill in the requested information as you read through procedures 1 through 8. The same procedures can be used to determine your 1RMs for other core exercises.

1. The chest exercise you have selected is _____.
2. Warm up by performing 1 set of 10 reps with your current 12-15RM load. Your current 12-15RM load is _____ pounds.
3. Add 10 pounds, or a weight-stack plate that is closest to equaling 10 pounds, and perform 3 reps. Your 12-15–pound load + 10 pounds = ___. Perform 3 reps with this load.
4. Add 10 more pounds, or the next heaviest weight-stack plate and, after resting 2-5 minutes, perform as many reps as possible. Give this your best effort!
   The load in procedure 3 = ____ + 10 pounds = ____.
   Perform as many reps as possible with this load.
5. Using Table 10.3, fill in the name of the exercise involved, the load used, and the reps completed.
6. Refer to Table 10.4, "Prediction of 1RM." Obtain and circle the "rep factor" associated with

the number of repetitions you completed with that load in the chest exercise.
7. Record the circled rep factor for your chest exercise in Table 10.3.
8. Multiply the rep factor by the load in this table to obtain the predicted 1RM for this exercise.

Figure 10.2 illustrates how Table 10.3 can be used with Table 10.4 to predict a 1RM in the next three procedures. In the example, 6 reps are performed with 120 pounds in the bench press exercise. The rep factor to the right of 6 reps is 1.20, which when multiplied by 120 equals 144 pounds, or 145 pounds (rounded off to the nearest 5 pounds or weight-stack plate).

Using the 1RM to Determine Training Loads

To use the 1RM to determine a training load, multiply the 1RM by a percentage. For example, if your 1RM in the standing press is 100 pounds, and you decide to use a 75 percent load, the training load would equal 1RM $\times$ 0.75 or 100 $\times$ 0.75 = 75 pounds. This will be discussed further in this step.

Table 10.4 Prediction of 1RM	
Reps completed	Rep factor
1	1.00
2	1.07
3	1.10
4	1.13
5	1.16
6	1.20
7	1.23
8	1.27
9	1.32
10	1.36

Note. From *Beginning Weight Training: The Safe and Effective Way* (p. 201) by V.P. Lombardi, 1989, Dubuque, IA: Brown. Copyright 1989 by William C. Brown. Adapted by permission.

Table 10.3   Developing the Chest 1RM Prediction Load

Core exercise name = *Bench press*

Reps completed = *6*

Rep factor

Load used x from Table 10.4 = Predicted 1RM

120 x *1.20* = *144*

Predicted 1RM rounded to the nearest 5 pounds/ weight-stack plate = 1RM of *145*

Number of reps performed

Rep factor for 6 reps

Figure 10.2   Predicting a 1RM.

1RM Load Self-Assessment Quiz

Answer the following questions by checking off the correct answer:

1. The load selected influences the [___ number ___ kind] of reps that are possible.
2. The load you select should also influence the [___ number of ___ length of the] rest periods between sets.
3. 1RM refers to [___ 1-repetition maximum ___ 1-minute rest minimum].

Self-Assessment Quiz Answers

1. **number**
2. **length of the**
3. **1-repetition maximum**

When and How Much to Increase Loads

It is important that you assume heavier loads as soon as you are able to complete the required number of reps. However, changes should not be made too soon. Wait until you can complete 2 or more reps above the intended number in the last set of two consecutive workouts (the 2-for-2 rule, Step 9). When you have met the 2-for-2 rule, instead of referring to the Load Adjustment Charts in Steps 3 through 8, simply increase loads by 2 1/2 or 5 pounds. The Load Adjustment Charts were used initially to assist primarily with large fluctuations in the number of reps performed. However, you will now find that fluctuations are much smaller, and that using the 2-for-2 rule with a 2 1/2- or 5-pound increase works well. There are two exceptions. In exercises involving large muscles (shoulder press, bench press, squat), you may need to make heavier increases. However, it is always better to underestimate than to overestimate the increase needed. The other exception concerns the use of smaller increments (2 1/2-pound) in arm (biceps, triceps, forearm) and neck exercises (using 1 1/4-pound plates). It is appropriate to use smaller load increments in exercises that involve smaller muscles. As training progresses, you may choose to vary the loads used in a different manner (and/or reps and sets performed).

Increasing Loads Self-Assessment Quiz

Answer the following questions by checking off the correct answer:

1. The 2-for-2 rule concerns [___ resting 2 minutes after every two exercises ___ completing 2 or more reps in the last set above the goal in two consecutive workouts before increasing the training load].
2. Load increases for the bench press and squat exercises are more likely to be [___ heavier ___ lighter] than those for the biceps and triceps exercises.

Self-Assessment Quiz Answers

1. **completing 2 or more reps in the last set for two consecutive workouts before increasing the training load**
2. **heavier**

Number of Reps to Perform

The number of reps you will be able to perform is directly related to the load you select. As the loads become heavier, the number of reps possible becomes fewer, and as the loads become lighter, the number of reps possible becomes greater. Assuming that a good effort is given in each set of exercises, the factor that dictates the number of reps is the load selected.

Number of Reps Self-Assessment Quiz

Answer the following questions by checking off the correct answer:

1. Heavier loads are associated with a [___ greater ___ fewer] number of reps.
2. The factor that dictates the number of reps completed is the [___ load ___ exercise] selected.

Self-Assessment Quiz Answers

1. **fewer**
2. **load**

Number of Sets

Some controversy exists as to whether multiple (2 or more) sets are better than single sets for developing strength, hypertrophy, and/or muscular endurance. While 1-set training works exceptionally well during the early stages (10 weeks), there is growing research that supports additional sets in the later stages of training. It seems reasonable to expect that the multiple-set approach to training provides a better stimulus for continued development. The rationale is that a single set of an exercise will not recruit all the fibers in a muscle and that performing additional sets will recruit more fibers. This is because muscle fibers that were involved in the first set will not be sufficiently recovered and, therefore, will rely on "fresh" fibers (not previously stimulated) for assistance. This is especially evident if an additional load is added to succeeding sets.

When 3 or more sets are performed, the likelihood of recruiting additional fibers becomes even greater. Further support for multiple sets comes from observations of the programs followed by successful competitive weightlifters, power lifters, and body builders. It is well known that these competitors rely on multiple sets for achieving high degrees of development. As you will see later, your goals for training should influence the number of sets you perform.

There is one more thing to consider. How much time do you have for training? For instance, if you choose to rest for 1 minute between exercises in your program (goal is hypertrophy), you should figure a minimum of 2 minutes per exercise (a minimum of 60 seconds to complete the reps in the exercise plus 60 seconds rest). Thus, your program of 7 exercises, in which you perform 1 set of each, should take 14 minutes. If you increase the number of sets to 2, and then to 3, your workout time will increase to 28 and 42 minutes, respectively. This assumes a 60-second rest period after each set. The actual time for rest between sets, as you will read soon, may vary between 30 seconds and 5 minutes.

Number of Sets Self-Assessment Quiz

Answer the following questions by checking off the correct answer:

1. The fewest number of sets recommended for continued development is [___ 1 ___ 2].
2. The basis for multiple-set training is that the additional sets are thought to [___ recruit ___ relax] a greater number of muscle fibers.

Self-Assessment Quiz Answers

1. **2**
2. **recruit**

Length of the Rest Period

The impact of the rest period between sets on the intensity of training is not usually recognized, but should be. Longer rest periods provide time for the "energizers" (phosphagens) of muscle contraction to rebuild, enabling muscles to exert greater force. If the amount of work is the same and the rest periods are shortened, the intensity of training increases. As you will soon read, the length of time between exercises or sets has a direct impact on the outcomes of training. A word of caution, however: Moving too rapidly from one exercise or set to another often reduces the number of reps you are able to perform (due to inadequate recovery time) and may cause you to become dizzy and nauseated.

Length of the Rest Period Self-Assessment Quiz

Answer the following questions by checking off the correct answer:

1. Longer rest periods enable you to exert [___ greater ___ lesser] force.
2. The length of the rest period has [___ an effect ___ no effect] on the outcome of training.

Self-Assessment Quiz Answers

1. **greater**
2. **an effect**

Application of the Specificity Concept

The earlier discussion of the specificity concept addressed only the issue of exercise selection, but this concept is broader in scope as it relates to program design. Table 10.5 shows how loads, reps, sets, and rest periods are manipulated using the specificity concept in designing three different programs: muscular endurance, hypertrophy, and strength. This table illustrates a continuum where the variable for the percentage of 1RM, number of reps and sets, and length of the rest period are presented. It reveals that muscular endurance programs (as compared to other programs) should include lighter loads (≤ 70 percent of 1RM), permit 12 to 20 reps, involve fewer sets (2 or 3), and have shorter rest periods (20 to 30 seconds). In contrast, programs designed to develop strength should include heavier loads (80 to 100 percent of 1RM) with fewer reps (1 to 8), more sets (3 to 5 or more), and longer rest periods between sets (2 to 5 minutes). Programs designed to develop hypertrophy (muscle size increases) should include reps, sets, and resting time variables that fall within the guidelines for muscle endurance and strength.

Programs based on these guidelines and designed specifically for developing muscular endurance, strength, or hypertrophy outcomes are discussed and illustrated in the following pages. They are basic introductory programs that you will want to refer to when completing Step 12.

Muscular Endurance Program

The program you have been following is designed to develop muscular endurance. You will notice some similarities between your program and the program for muscular endurance in Table 10.5. The loads you are using now may permit you to perform 15, but not quite 20, reps. Also, your rest periods are close to the suggested 30 seconds if you have made an effort to shorten them. If you choose in Step 12 to continue with your muscular endurance program, do not increase the load until you are able to perform 20 reps in the last set in two consecutive workouts, and keep the rest periods at 20 to 30 seconds. Except for specific situations, such as training for competitive endurance events, rest periods less than 30 seconds are not recommended.

Muscular Endurance Program Self-Assessment Quiz

Answer the following questions:

1. The guidelines to use when designing your program for muscular endurance are as follows:
   a. Relative loading = ____
   b. Percentage of 1RM load = ____
   c. Repetition range = ____
   d. Number of sets = ____
2. Unless there is a specific reason, the appropriate amount of rest between sets and exercises in a muscular endurance program is [___ 45 seconds ___ 30 seconds].

Self-Assessment Quiz Answers

1. **a. light b. 60 to 70 percent c. 12 to 20 d. 2 or 3**
2. **30 seconds**

Hypertrophy Programs

If you decide in Step 12 to emphasize hypertrophy, review the guidelines in Table 10.5 and consider the example in Table 10.6, where 1RM = 100 pounds, when modifying your program.

The keys of a successful hypertrophy program appear to be associated with the use of moderate loads—70 to 80 percent of 1RM; a medium number of reps (8-12) per set; between 3-6 sets; and moderate rest periods—30-90 seconds between exercise sets. A simple method for establishing 70-80 percent loads is to add 5 pounds to what you are using. Do this only with the core exercises; keep the loads for other exercises the same and apply the 2-for-2 rule when making load adjustments. You will observe that successful body builders usually do not rest long between sets and that they perform a lot of sets. Thus, they combine the multiple-set program described earlier in this step with the rest period and load guidelines presented in Table 10.5 to promote improvements in hypertrophy.

Two unique methods implemented in hypertrophy programs are the super set and the compound set. A *super set* occurs when the individual performs two exercises that train opposing muscle groups without rest between the two exercises—for example, 1 set of biceps curls followed immediately by 1 set of triceps extensions. Consecutively completing two exercises that train the same muscle group without rest between them is termed a *compound set*. An example of this is to perform 1 set of barbell biceps curls followed immediately by dumbbell biceps curls. The fact that these approaches deviate from the rest periods shown in Table 10.5 certainly does not mean that such approaches are ineffective. The time frames

Table 10.5 Specificity Concept Applied to Program Design Variables					
Relative loading	Outcome of training	% 1RM	Rep range	# of sets	Rest between sets
Light	Muscular endurance	60-70	12-20	2-3	20-30 seconds
Moderate	Hypertrophy	70-80	8-12	3-6	30-90 seconds
Heavy	Strength	80-100	1-8	3-5+	2-5 minutes

Table 10.6 Example: Hypertrophy Program Multiple Set–Same Load Training (1RM = 100 pounds)			
Set	% 1RM	Weight/resistance pounds	Reps
1	75	75	8-12
2		same % load	8-12
3		same % load	8-12
Length of rest between sets = 30-90 seconds			

indicated are only guidelines. There are many ways to manipulate program design variables to produce positive outcomes.

Hypertrophy Program Self-Assessment Quiz

Answer the following questions:

1. The guidelines to use when designing your program so that hypertrophy is the outcome are as follows:
   a. Relative loading = ____
   b. Percentage of 1RM load = ____
   c. Repetition range = ____
   d. Number of sets = ____
   e. Rest period = ____
2. Given a 1RM of 100 pounds, a 75-pound load is associated with achieving the goals of a [__ strength __ hypertrophy __ muscular endurance] program.
3. When opposing muscle groups are exercised without rest, this arrangement is referred to as a [__ super set __ compound set].

Self-Assessment Quiz Answers

1. a. moderate b. 70 to 80 percent c. 8 to 12 d. 3 to 6 e. 30 to 90 seconds
2. hypertrophy
3. super set

Strength Programs

There are many ways to approach programs designed to produce significant strength gains. The two presented here are commonly used by successful power lifters and weightlifters, and apply best to large-muscle (core) exercises.

Pyramid Training

If you decide in Step 12 to change your program to emphasize strength development, one method of applying the guidelines presented in Table 10.5 can be seen in Table 10.7. The example uses a predicted 1RM of 150 pounds in the bench press exercise. To bring about the proper loading to produce the goal of 6 to 8 reps in the first set, use 80 percent of the 1RM. This percentage will equal 120 pounds (150 × 0.80 = 120). Another method that will get you close to an 80 percent of 1RM load is to add 10 to 15 pounds to what you are using in your core exercises. Remember to keep other exercise loads the same and apply the 2-for-2 rule when making load adjustments.

Now, to incorporate the concept of progressive overload, you can use what is referred to as light to heavy pyramid training, where each succeeding set becomes heavier. Increase the 80 percent 1RM (120 pounds) load to equal approximately 85 percent of the 1RM (130 pounds) in the second set, and to 90 percent of the 1RM (135 pounds) in the third set. Note that sometimes you will need to round off loads to the nearest 5 pounds/weight stack-plate, as has been done with the 85 percent load in set 2. If 5 sets are to be performed, increase the load to equal 95 percent of the 1RM for the fourth and fifth sets. Between each set, rest 2 or more minutes. Do not be surprised when the number of reps decrease as you continue from set 1 to 2, set 2 to 3, and so on. In fact, the load increases are designed to decrease the number of reps: from 6 to 8 in set 1, 4 to 7 in set 2, 1 to 3 in set 3 (and 1 or 2 in sets 4 and 5 in more advanced training programs). Use this approach with large-muscle (core) exercises, while performing 3 sets of 8-12 reps in other exercises. Heavy loads tend to produce too much stress on the smaller muscles and joints.

Forcing yourself to train to the point of muscular failure while using progressively heavier poundages from set to set (progressive overload principle) will provide the stimulus for dramatic strength gains. As training sessions continue, the need to add weight to one or more successive sets will be a natural outcome. As training continues and the intensity of workouts increases, there will be a time when training to muscular failure is appropriate only in certain exercises and on designated days. This is discussed in Step 12.

Multiple Sets–Same Load Training

Another popular approach used to develop strength is to perform 3 to 5 sets of 2 to 8 reps with the same load in the core exercises and 3 sets of 8 to 12 reps in other exercises, as shown in Table 10.8. The program can be made more aggressive by decreasing the goal reps—which means you must use heavier loads (6 reps = 85 percent, 4 = 90 percent, 2 = 95 percent of the 1RM). Notice how the percentage of the 1RM is associated with the goal reps of 6, 4, and 2 at the bottom of this table. You will find that completing the specified number of reps in set 1 is usually easy, set 2 is more difficult, and set 3 is very difficult, if not impossible. With continued training, sets 2 and 3 will become easier, and eventually you will need to increase loads. As already mentioned, keeping the loads the same in several sets of the same exercise is also a popular training approach among body builders. The difference here is that the loads used for developing strength are heavier and the rest periods are longer.

Table 10.7   Example: Strength Program Pyramid Training and Use of the 1RM (1RM in bench press = 150 pounds)

Set	1RM x % 1RM = Load	Goal reps
Warm-up	Use present training load	10
1	150 x .80% = 120 Training load = 120 pounds	6-8
2	150 x .85% = 130 Training load = 130 pounds	4-7
3	150 x .90% = 135 Training load = 135 pounds	2-3
	Length of rest between sets = 2-5 minutes	

Table 10.8   Example: Strength Program Multiple Sets–Same Load Training (1RM in bench press = 150 pounds)

Set	1RM	Core exercises			Load	Goal reps
		x	% 1RM	=		
1	150	x	.80	=	120	8
2	150	x	.80	=	120	8
3	150	x	.80	=	120	8
	Use .85% 1RM for goal reps of 6					
	Use .90% 1RM for goal reps of 4					
	Use .95% 1RM for goal reps of 2					
	(Other exercises: 3 sets of 8-12 reps)					

Strength Program Self-Assessment Quiz

Answer the following questions (check off two answers for question 4):

1. The guidelines to use when designing your program so that strength is the outcome are as follows:
   a. Relative loading = ___
   b. Percentage of 1RM load = ___
   c. Repetition range = ___
   d. Number of sets = ___
   e. Rest period = ___
2. Given a 1RM of 200 pounds and a goal of strength development, the lightest load for a first set should be [___ 160 pounds ___ 140 pounds].
3. The use of progressively heavier poundages in each set of the pyramid training approach demonstrates the use of the [___ 2-for-2 ___ overload principle].
4. The two strength development programs described here have been referred to as [___ 1RM ___ pyramid ___ multiple set–same load ___ overload].
5. Heavier loads are not used with [___ smaller ___ larger] muscle groups because that method of training imposes too much stress on the involved muscle and joint structures.

Self-Assessment Quiz Answers

1. a. heavy b. 80 to 100 percent c. 1 to 8 d. 3 to 5 e. 2 to 5 minutes
2. 160 pounds
3. overload principle
4. pyramid, multiple set–same load
5. smaller

MANIPULATING PROGRAM DESIGN VARIABLES

DRILLS

1. Loads, Reps, Sets, and Rest Period Drill

You have had an opportunity to learn about how the specificity concept and overload principle are used in determining loads, the implications of these loads on the number of reps and sets, and the length of the rest periods between exercises and sets. As a review, fill in the missing information in Table 10.9.

Relative loading	Outcome of training	% 1RM	Rep range	# of sets	Rest between sets
Table 10.9 Specificity Concept Applied to Program Design Variables					
_____	Strength	_____	1-8	_____	2-5 minutes
Moderate	_____	70-80	_____	3-6	_____
_____	Muscular endurance	_____	12-20	_____	20-30 seconds

Success Goal = 9 blanks in Table 10.9 are correctly filled in ___

Success Check

- Apply the specificity concept and overload principle in determining percentage of the 1RM answers ___
- Apply the specificity concept in determining answers to repetition question ___
- Apply the overload principle in determining answers to number of sets questions ___
- Apply the specificity concept and overload principle in determining answers to the number of sets ___
- Apply the specificity concept in determining the length of rest period ___

2. Determining Load Ranges

This drill will give you experience in determining training loads using either a predicted or actual 1RM, and in applying the knowledge you have gained concerning training load ranges. Using 80 pounds as the 1RM and the example shown for a hypertrophy program, determine the training load ranges for a strength and endurance program. Remember to round off numbers to the nearest 5 pounds or closest weight-stack plate. Write your answers in the blanks below the "Training Load Ranges" heading.

Goal	1RM	×	Training Load (%)	=	Training Load Ranges*
Hypertrophy: *Example:*	80	×	70 to 80%	=	60 to 65 pounds
Strength:	80		___ %	=	___ to ___ pounds
Muscular endurance:	80		___ %	=	___ to ___ pounds

*Rounded off to the nearest 5 pounds or weight-stack plate.

Success Goal =

a. 2 training load percents are correctly recorded ___
b. 4 training loads are correctly recorded ___

Success Check

- Remember relative percents for specific training outcomes ___
- Round off value to nearest 5 pounds or closest weight stack ___

Self-Assessment Quiz Answers

Strength: **80 to 100; 65 to 80**
Muscular endurance: **60 to 70; 50 to 60**

Deciding Training Frequency

Training frequency and program variation are the last program design variables to be covered before you are challenged to design your own program. Essentially, the questions that need to be answered are (a) How often should you train? and (b) How should you change the program so improvement continues?

Frequency of Training

The frequency of your training, just like the application of the overload principle, is an essential element in establishing the proper intensity in successful programs. To be effective, training must occur on a regular basis. Sporadic training short-circuits your body's ability to adapt. But also realize that rest between training days is just as important as the actual training! Your body needs time to recover, that is time to move the waste products of exercise out of the muscle and nutrients in so that muscles torn down from training can rebuild and thus increase in size and strength. Rest and nutritious food intake are essential to muscle's continued growth. Often individuals who are new to weight training become so excited with the changes in their strength and appearance that they come in to train on the scheduled rest days. *More is not always better*, especially during the beginning stages of your program!

3-Days-a-Week Programs

Allow at least 48 hours before you train the same muscle again, which usually means training 3 days a week. Typically, this means training on Monday, Wednesday, and Friday; Tuesday, Thursday, and Saturday; or Sunday, Tuesday, and Thursday. In a 3-days-a-week program, all exercises are performed each training day.

Split Programs

A split program is a more advanced method of training that typically involves splitting up a program of exercises and performing part of them 2 days a week (e.g., Monday and Thursday) and the rest on 2 different days (e.g., Tuesday and Friday). A split program typically involves more exercises and sets and has the 4 training days scheduled, as shown in Table

Table 10.10 4-Days-a-Week Split Training Program			
OPTION A		OPTION B	
Exercise	Type	Exercise	Type
Monday and Thursday (Upper body)		**Monday and Thursday** (Chest, shoulders, and arms)	
Bench press	Push	Bench press	Push
Lat pull-down	Pull	Biceps curl	Pull
Dumbbell fly	Push	Standing press	Push
Biceps curl	Pull	Abdominal crunch	Pull
Standing press	Push	Triceps extension	Push
Abdominal crunch	Pull		
Triceps extension	Push		
Tuesday and Friday (Lower body)		**Tuesday and Friday** (Legs and back)	
Lunge	Push	Bent over row	Pull
Leg curl	Pull	Leg press	Push
Leg extension	Push	Leg curl	Pull
Bent-knee sit-up	Pull	Leg extension	Push
Seated toe raise	Push	Bent-knee sit-up	Pull

10.10. On the left half of this table (Option A) exercises are split into upper body and lower body, with abdominal exercises on all training days. Option B in the right half of this table illustrates another common split program option, where exercises for the chest, shoulders, and arms are "split" from leg and back exercises and are performed on different days. Abdominal exercises are performed on all training days. Notice that an effort has been made in both options to arrange exercises so that pushing and pulling exercises are alternated and triceps and biceps exercises are located after upper body pressing and pulling movements, respectively.

The split program offers several advantages. It spreads the exercises in your workout over 4 instead of 3 days, thereby usually reducing the amount of time required to complete each workout. This offers the opportunity to add more exercises and sets while keeping workout time reasonable. Because you can add more exercises, you are able to emphasize muscular development in specific muscle groups, should you decide to do so. Its disadvantage is that you must train 4 instead of 3 days a week.

Frequency of Training Self-Assessment Quiz

Answer the following questions by checking off the correct answer:

1. Establishing the proper stimulus for improvement is dependent upon use of the overload principle and training [___ on a regular basis ___ in a sporadic manner].
2. Compared to a split program, the 3-days-a-week program typically includes a [___ greater ___ fewer] number of exercises.
3. Compared to the 3-days-a-week program, the workouts in a split program usually take [___ less ___ more] time to complete.
4. The [___ split ___ 3-days-a-week program] offers the best opportunity for emphasizing development in specific muscle areas.

Self-Assessment Quiz Answers

1. **on a regular basis**
2. **fewer**
3. **less**
4. **split**

PROGRAM DESIGN CONSIDERATIONS SUCCESS SUMMARY

A clear understanding of how to apply the specificity concept and the overload principle is the basis for well-conceived programs. Understanding and incorporating the loads, reps, sets, and rest period length guidelines for muscular endurance, hypertrophy, and strength programs are the keys to developing programs that meet your specific needs. When selecting exercises, keep in mind the specificity concept and the equipment and spotter requirements for each exercise. Also, include at least one exercise for each large muscle area, and remember the need to select balanced pairs of exercises. Include additional exercises if you want to emphasize the development of certain muscle areas, but not so many that workouts take too long. Last, remember that how you arrange exercises and the order in which you actually perform them also has a direct impact on your success.

Training on a regular basis is essential to the success of your weight training program. Beginning programs typically begin with 2 or 3 workout days a week, and may evolve into 4-days-a-week split programs. The greater time commitment in split programs is offset by the advantages of being able to emphasize certain body parts (because of the extra training time). Your ability to recover from workout sessions is critical to your future training successes; more is not always better. Last, muscles need to be nourished, especially after a challenging workout. Eating nutritious meals is essential for muscle repair and size and strength increases.

STEP 11

MAXIMIZE TRAINING OUTCOMES: ADJUSTING INTENSITIES

This step builds upon the discussion of exercise selection, loads, reps, sets, rest periods, and training frequency variables in Step 10 and describes how these program design variables can be manipulated to maximize training outcomes.

Why Adjust Training Intensity?

If you perform the same number of sets and reps on the same days each week and with the same loads week after week, a plateau in strength will occur and your goals for training will not be realized. Thus, program design variables need to be systematically varied or manipulated in order to promote continued improvement and to avoid overtraining (discussed in the "Physiological Considerations" section, page 3).

While there is a need to perform greater numbers of reps and sets and use heavier loads for improvement to continue, too many reps and sets performed with aggressive loads and without adequate rest periods can result in extended periods of muscle soreness, aggravate existing joint problems, and result in injury. The goal, therefore, is to design programs that vary the overall intensity of training, providing both the needed overload as well as the rest needed to bring about maximum gains without injury.

Training Variation

Training variation involves systematically manipulating the variables of

- training frequency,
- exercises selected,
- arrangement of exercises,
- number of reps per set,
- number of sets, and the

- length of the rest periods between workout sessions.

Program approaches designed to vary the intensity of training pay special attention to the loads assumed by large muscle groups (leg, shoulder, chest) in core exercises (discussed in Step 10). It is believed that the larger muscle mass and the joint structures of the larger muscle groups make them better suited to withstand the rigors of training than the smaller groups. You may recall from the previous step that the large muscle groups were identified as being appropriate for the heavier loads assumed in the pyramid (strength development) program, for the same reason.

Some of the common approaches used to vary the intensity of workouts are to

- use heavy, light, and medium-heavy loads on different days of the week;
- increase loads from week to week; or
- change loads in a cyclical manner every 2 or more weeks.

The approaches here concern *only* the core exercises and are most applicable to programs involving 3 or more sets and those designed for strength development and hypertrophy. The loads used in the noncore exercises should continue to yield 8 to 12 reps, and these loads should be gradually increased using the 2-for-2 rule. Although the discussion here focuses on the loads used, you should realize that the number of reps and sets may also be manipulated (and usually are) to vary training intensities.

Within-the-Week Variations

Three different ways to increase loads within a week follow.

3-Days-a-Week–Same-Load-in-Sets

Table 11.1 shows you an example of a 3-days-a-week workout program where heavy (H), light (L), and medium-heavy (MH) loads are varied within the week. The loads used in a particular day's workout stay the same (they are not increased, thus the "same-load-in-sets" approach name). The 2 × 8-12 means 2 sets of 8 to 12 reps; 3 sets of 8 to 10 reps would be written 3 × 8-10. If you perform 3 sets of 8-10 reps with 120 pounds, you would write it like this: 120 × 3 × 8-10.

Notice that in these tables only exercises for the larger muscles (core) are associated with the letters H, MH, or L, designating the use of heavy (85 percent of 1RM), medium-heavy (80 percent of 1RM), and light (70 percent of 1RM) loads, respectively. Other exercises involve loads permitting 8 to 12 reps. Even though you may be able to, do not perform more than 10 reps on your light (L) day (Wednesday) and 8

reps on your medium-heavy day (Friday). Notice that Monday, the more intense training day, is followed by the least intense training day, which is then followed by a medium-intensity day, so that your body has a chance to recover. You will see this pattern repeat itself in all the training program examples provided in this step.

3-Days-a-Week Pyramid

In Step 10 you learned about the use of the pyramid approach, where progressive load increases occur from one set to another until all sets for a specific exercise are completed. In Table 11.2 you will recognize these progressive increases, but also realize that the loads used vary from 80 to 90 percent of 1RM on Monday (H), from 70 to 80 percent on Wednesday (L), and from 75 to 85 percent on Friday (MH). The example uses a 1RM of 150 pounds.

Table 11.1   Within-Week Training Load Variation (3-Days-a-Week–Same-Load-in-Sets Approach)

Exercise	Monday	Wednesday	Friday
Chest press**	H 3 x 3-8	L 3 x 10	MH 3 x 6-8
Bent over row	2 x 8-12	2 x 8-12	2 x 8-12
Standing press**	H 3 x 3-8	L 3 x 10	MH 3 x 6-8
Biceps curl	2 x 8-12	2 x 8-12	2 x 8-12
Triceps extension	2 x 8-12	2 x 8-12	2 x 8-12
Back squat**	H 3 x 3-8	L 3 x 10	MH 3 x 6-8
Abdominal crunch or sit-up	2 x 15-30 reps each day		

Explanation of loads: H (Heavy) = 85% 1RM, L (Light) = 70% 1RM, MH (Medium-Heavy) = 80% 1RM

**Core exercises, 3-5 sets

Table 11.2   3-Days-a-Week Pyramid Approach Within-Week Methods of Varying Loads (Current predicted 1RM = 150 pounds)

MONDAY-HEAVY (H)				WEDNESDAY-LIGHT (L)				FRIDAY-MEDIUM-HEAVY (MH)			
% 1RM	Load (lb)	# Sets	Reps	% 1RM	Load (lb)	# Sets	Reps	% 1RM	Load (lb)	# Sets	Reps
80	120 x	1 x	6-8	70	105 x	1 x	10	75	115 x	1 x	8
85	130 x	1 x	4-7	75	115 x	1 x	8	80	125 x	1 x	6
90	135 x	1 x	1-3	80	120 x	1 x	6	85	130 x	1 x	4

4-Days-a-Week–Heavy-Light Split Program

Table 11.3, a and b, shows how a 4-days-a-week split program might be organized to vary heavy and light loads within the week. Table 11.3a shows the assignment of loads on Monday and Thursday for the chest, shoulder, and arm exercises. Table 11.3b shows load assignments on Tuesday and Friday for the back and leg exercises.

Week-to-Week Variations

Two ways to increase loads on a weekly basis are shown in Table 11.4. Option A involves simply scheduling a 3 percent increase in the training load each week. Option B also shows a 3 percent increase (Monday) each week, followed by the use of light and medium-heavy loads on Wednesday and Friday, respectively.

Cyclical Training Variations

The previously explained approaches provide variations in the intensity of training. If, however, you were to continue following such programs for an extended period of time, a plateau or an overtraining injury would most likely be the outcome. You will recall the earlier emphasis on the need for proper rest. Programs that continue to increase loads (and reps or sets) without scheduling rest time will not produce optimal gains. The term *cycling* here refers to the scheduling of cycles of high-intensity with low-intensity training periods.

Table 11.5 represents a 7-week cycle that includes load variations within the week, and load and set increases every 3 weeks of training. Following Table 11.5 is an explanation of the 7-week cycle. Notice that the seventh week involves lighter loads and fewer

Table 11.3a Monday-Thursday Split Program (Chest, Shoulders, and Arms)		
Exercise	Monday	Thursday
Chest press**	H	L
Biceps curl	4 x 8-12	4 x 8-12
Standing press**	H	L
Triceps extension	4 x 8-12	4 x 8-12
Abdominal crunch	2 x 15-30 reps each day	
H = 80-90% 1RM, L = 60-70% 1RM, MH = 70-80% 1RM ** = Core exercises		

Table 11.3b Tuesday-Friday Split Program (Back and Legs)		
Exercise	Tuesday	Friday
Back squat**	H	L
Bent over row	4 x 8-12	4 x 8-12
Abdominal crunch	2 x 15-30 reps each day	
H = 80-90% 1RM, L = 60-70% 1RM, MH = 70-80% 1RM ** = Core exercises		

sets (less intensive workouts), providing an opportunity for the body to recover and to make jumps over previous strength levels in succeeding weeks. Load increases that occur after the third and sixth weeks are determined by the number of reps completed during the Friday workouts of those weeks. The number of sets may also be increased after each 3-week period. A 4-days-a-week program could be cycled in a similar way. The decision to increase the number of sets to 5 or 6 after a 7-week cycle should be based upon how well you are able to recover from your program and how much time you have for training.

That is, a new 1RM is determined for core exercises using the method described on page 138 for determining loads that should be used during the following week's workouts. In the other exercises, continue to use the 2-for-2 rule to make needed load increases.

Table 11.4   Within- and Between-Weeks Load Variations

Option A   Same loads within the week, increases between weeks

Week	Monday % 1RM	Wednesday % 1RM	Friday % 1RM
1	80	80	80
2	83	83	83
3	86	86	86

Option B   Within- and between-week load variations

Week	Monday % 1RM	Wednesday % 1RM	Friday % 1RM
1	80	70	75
2	83	73	78
3	86	76	81

Table 11.5   7-Week Training Cycle

Week	Sets	Monday	Wednesday	Friday
1	3	H*	L	MH
2	3	H	L	MH
3	3	MH	L	Test
4	4	H*	L	MH
5	4	H	L	MH
6	4	MH	L	Test
7	2	L	L	L
8-14	Repeat 7-week cycle with new training loads			

H = 80% 1RM, L = 70% 1RM, MH = 75% 1RM

* Indicates that new loads are used

7-Week Training Cycle Explained

Weeks 1 and 2

Core exercises:

Monday workouts—perform as many reps as possible.

Wednesday and Friday workouts—reps stay within recommended ranges.

Other exercises:

Perform as many reps as possible, and increase loads using the 2-for-2 rule.

Abdominal exercises—perform 15 to 30 reps per workout.

Week 3

Core exercises:

Monday workout—use medium-heavy loads.

Wednesday—use light loads.

Friday—test on your third set, and calculate your new training load.

Other exercises:

Perform as many reps as possible, and increase loads using the 2-for-2 rule.

Abdominal exercises—perform 15 to 30 reps per workout.

Weeks 4 and 5

Start as the first week, but with new training loads.

Week 6

Test again and calculate new training loads.

Week 7

Use light (new) loads for 2 sets in all exercises this week.

Week 8

Repeat 7-week cycle with new training loads.

Procedures for Testing on the Third and Sixth Weeks of the 7-Week Cycle

Use the following procedures on the Friday of each third week of the training period to determine new training loads. Notice that a shortcut for identifying training loads is also explained.

1. Warm up as usual, then use Friday's loads in sets 1 and 2, but perform only 5 and 3 reps, respectively.

2a. If you are using the pyramid method, perform as many reps as possible with the heaviest load used thus far in this cycle.

2b. If you are using the "same-load-in-each-set" method, increase the load by 10 pounds and perform as many reps as possible.

3. Predict the 1RM using the procedures you learned in Step 10.

Shortcut for Determining Training Loads

Instead of multiplying the predicted 1RM by the desired training percentage as you did in Step 10 to determine training loads, refer to Table 11.6 and follow these procedures:

1. Refer to Table 11.6 and in the far left-hand 1RM column locate and circle your predicted value.

2. Identify the desired training percentage (50 to 95 percent) column.

3. Follow the percentage column down until it parallels the location of your predicted 1RM value.

4. Circle where these two points converge. The number you circle is your training load.

The example in Figure 11.1 is of someone who completed 7 reps with 90 pounds and wants a training load that represents 85 percent of 1RM. Performing 7 reps with 90 pounds equals a 1RM of 110 pounds using the "Prediction of 1RM" in Step 10. Notice that in Table 11.6 under the column heading "1RM" that 110 pounds is found on line 9. Where line 9 and the 85 percent column converge is the load you should use. The number 94 is rounded to the nearest 5 pounds or weight-stack plate, which is 95 pounds in this example.

Whatever method is chosen to create variations in intensity, you should perform as many reps as possible on the heavy day of your workout in the core exercises, but keep the reps within the designated ranges during the Wednesday and Friday workouts. This means that even though you are capable of performing more reps with the lighter Wednesday and Friday loads—don't! In the other (noncore) exercises, perform as many reps as possible in all workouts, and use the 2-for-2 rule for increasing loads.

						Training load percentages				
	1RM	50%	60%	70%	75%	80%	85%	90%	95%
1.	30	15	18	21	23	24	26	27	29
2.	40	20	24	28	30	32	34	36	38
3.	50	25	30	35	38	40	43	45	48
4.	60	30	36	42	45	48	51	54	57
5.	70	35	42	49	52	56	60	63	67
6.	80	40	48	56	60	64	68	72	76
7.	90	45	54	63	68	72	77	81	86
8.	100	50	60	70	75	80	85	90	95
9.	110	55	66	77	83	88	94	99	105
10.	120	60	72	84	90	96	102	108	114
11.	130	65	78	91	98	104	111	117	124
12.	140	70	84	98	105	112	119	125	133
13.	150	75	90	105	113	120	128	135	143
14.	160	80	96	112	120	128	136	144	152
15.	170	85	102	119	128	136	145	153	162
16.	180	90	108	126	135	144	153	162	171
17.	190	95	114	133	143	152	162	171	181
18.	200	100	120	140	150	160	170	180	190
19.	210	105	126	147	158	168	179	189	200
20.	220	110	132	154	165	176	187	198	209
21.	230	115	138	161	173	184	196	207	219
22.	240	120	144	168	180	192	204	216	228
23.	250	125	150	175	188	200	213	225	238
24.	260	130	156	182	195	208	221	234	247
25.	270	135	162	189	203	216	230	243	257
26.	280	140	168	196	210	224	238	252	266
27.	290	145	174	203	218	232	247	261	276
28.	300	150	180	210	225	240	255	270	285
29.	310	155	186	217	233	248	264	279	295
30.	320	160	192	224	240	256	272	288	304
31.	330	165	198	231	248	264	281	297	314
32.	340	170	204	238	255	272	289	306	323
33.	350	175	210	245	263	280	298	316	333
34.	360	180	216	252	278	288	306	324	342
35.	370	185	222	259	280	296	315	333	352
36.	380	190	228	266	285	304	323	342	361
37.	390	195	234	273	293	312	332	351	371
38.	400	200	240	280	300	320	340	360	380

Table 11.6 **Training Load Determination**

Program Variation Self-Assessment Quiz

Answer the following questions by checking off the correct answer:

1. The reps performed on light and medium-heavy training days provide the opportunity for you to [___ apply the overload principle ___ recover from the overloading].

2. You should perform [___ the designated number of reps ___ as many reps as possible] on heavy training days.

3. The two variables that have been manipulated in the 7-week cycle program in Table 11.5 are [___ reps and sets ___ loads and sets].

Self-Assessment Quiz Answers

1. recover from the overloading
2. as many reps as possible
3. loads and sets

Table 10.4 Prediction of 1RM	
Reps completed	Rep factor
1	1.00
2	1.07
3	1.10
4	1.13
5	1.16
6	1.20
⑦ reps = → (1.23) → x 90 = (110 pounds) (rounded)	1.23
8	1.27
9	1.32
10	1.36

Note. From *Beginning Weight Training: The Safe and Effective Way* (p. 201) by V.P. Lombardi, 1989, Dubuque, IA: Brown. Copyright 1989 by William C. Brown. Adapted by permission.

94 rounded to the nearest 5 pounds = 95 pound training load

		Table 11.6 Training Load Determination				
			Training load percentages			
	1RM	50%	60%	70%	75%	80%	85%
1.	30	15	18	21	23	24	26
2.	40	20	24	28	30	32	34
3.	50	25	30	35	38	40	43
4.	60	30	36	42	45	48	51
5.	70	35	42	49	52	56	60
6.	80	40	48	56	60	64	68
7.	90	45	54	63	68	72	77
8.	100	50	60	70	75	80	85
9.	110	55	66	77	83	88	94
10.	120	60	72	84	90	96	102
11.	130	65	78	91	98	104	111
12.	140	70	84	98	105	112	119
13.	150	75	90	105	113	120	128
14.	160	80	96	112	120	128	136
15.	170	85	102	119	128	136	145
16.	180	90	108	126	135	144	153
17.	190	95	114	133	143	152	162
18.	200	100	120	140	150	160	170
19.	210	105	126	147	158	168	179
20.	220	110	132	154	165	176	1
21.	230	115	138	161	173	184	
22.	240	120	144	168	180	192	
23.	250	125	150	175	188	200	
24.	260	130	156	182	195	208	

Figure 11.1   A shortcut for determining training loads.

DRILLS

1. Shortcut Method

This drill is designed to give you experience in the shortcut method of determining training loads using Table 11.6. Assume that you performed 8 reps with 150 pounds and want to identify a training load that represents 75 percent of 1RM. What is the correct load? Remember to use the "Prediction of 1RM" Table 10.4 first, then use this 1RM value and the 75% 1RM column to locate the correct training load. Round off this value to the nearest 5-pound increment or weight-stack plate.

Success Goal = 145 pounds is determined to be the training load ___

Success Check
• Use Tables 10.4 and 11.6 ___
• Associate reps completed with rep factor ___
• Multiply rep factor by load ___
• Identify intersecting point in Table 11.6 ___

Explanation for Training Load Answer

Training load = 145 pounds. The rep factor from Table 10.4 for 8 reps = 1.27; 150 pounds × 1.27 = 190.5 pounds; 190 pounds (1RM) is located on line 17 in Table 11.6. Where line 17 intersects with the 75 percent column is the number 143. Rounded off, this number equals the training load of 145 pounds.

2. Determining Training Loads in a Program

To give you another opportunity to determine training loads using Table 11.6 and the prediction of the 1RM table, fill in training loads for the program in Table 11.7a. In this drill assume that 5 reps have been performed with 100 pounds.

Success Goal = 9 loads are correctly calculated in Table 11.7a ___

Success Check
• Remember to round off loads ___
• Refer to previous drill if needed ___

Table 11.7a Determining Loads in a Program						
	Monday		Wednesday		Friday	
Week	% 1RM	# Sets	% 1RM	# Sets	% 1RM	# Sets
1	80 = ____	5	70 = ____	3	75 = ____	4
2	80 = ____	5	70 = ____	3	75 = ____	4
3	80 = ____	5	70 = ____	3	75 = ____	4

Answers to Determining Training Loads

After you have completed this drill, refer to Table 11.7b to check your answers.

Table 11.7b	Answers to Determining Loads in a Program						
	Monday		**Wednesday**		**Friday**	
Week	% 1RM	# Sets	% 1RM	# Sets	% 1RM	# Sets
1	80 = 95	5	70 = 85	3	75 = 90	4
2	80 = 95	5	70 = 85	3	75 = 90	4
3	80 = 95	5	70 = 85	3	75 = 90	4

Note that load used = 100 x rep factor of 1.16 (for 5 reps) = 116.
116 rounded = 120 pounds for the predicted 1RM, which is line 10 in Table 11.6.
120 x .80 = 96 pounds (round to 95), 120 x .70 = 84 pounds (round to 85), and 120 x .75 = 90 pounds.

MAXIMIZE TRAINING OUTCOMES SUCCESS SUMMARY

There are many ways to vary the intensity of training, the most common of which involves manipulating the amount of the load, the number of sets and reps, and the number of training days. The use of cycling programs that include aggressive training weeks followed by a week (or weeks) of less aggressive training provides an appropriate overload stimulus and an opportunity for the body to recover and make significant gains. As you become more experienced, you will want to learn more about the cycling concept. Excellent discussions of this approach are presented by Baechle (1994), Baechle and Groves (1994), Baechle and Earle (1995), Fleck and Kraemer (1997), and Lombardi (1989).

STEP 12

YOUR PERSONALIZED PROGRAM: PUTTING IT ALL TOGETHER

N ow you will have a chance to apply all that you have learned in this text and develop your own weight training program. You will be prompted to use the knowledge acquired concerning the program design variables in the last two steps and to apply the overload and specificity concepts in designing a program that meets your specific needs. Follow the order of the tasks presented. After completing all the tasks in this step you will have developed a well-conceived weight training program that meets your specific needs. You may also use these tasks as a self-assessment of the knowledge you have acquired from this text on how to design a weight training program.

Follow this order when tailoring your program:

1. Determine your goals.
2. Select exercises.
3. Decide on frequency of training.
4. Arrange exercises in the workout.
5. Decide which loads to use.
6. Decide how many reps to perform.
7. Decide how many sets of each exercise to perform.
8. Decide on length of rest periods.
9. Decide how to vary the program.

1. Determine Your Goals

Decide on and place a check mark in the parentheses by one or more of the following training goals that apply. Then read the section that follows, which briefly explains how to accomplish each goal. My goal(s) for training are

( ) Muscular endurance

( ) Hypertrophy

( ) Strength

( ) Strength and hypertrophy

( ) General muscle toning

( ) Body composition (reproportioning)

( ) Other (list)

If Your Goal Is Muscular Endurance

As you have learned earlier, your present program is designed to improve muscular endurance. If this is the outcome you want from training, you will not need to change what you are doing to any great extent. Simply try to increase the number of reps from 15 to 20 in core exercises, and increase the number of sets. More changes, however, are indicated if hypertrophy, strength, combinations of hypertrophy and strength, or reproportioning are the desired outcomes.

If Your Goal Is Hypertrophy

To produce hypertrophy, you need to use loads that are slightly heavier than those that resulted in 12-15 reps. The loads you select should now keep your reps between 8 and 12. You probably will also need to include a good number of exercises and sets. You may want to initially focus on chest and arm development. Avoid the common tendency, however, of spending too much time on these body parts at the exclusion of your legs. Also realize that as you increase the number of exercises, sets (to as many as 6), and days of training, the amount of time that you will need to commit will increase substantially (1-1/2 to 2-1/2 hours, three or four times a week).

If Your Goal Is Strength

If strength is your goal you will need to use loads that are quite a bit heavier than you are currently using. An important thing to remember (from Step

143

10) is that to safely and effectively handle the heavier loads associated with developing strength, you must have fairly long rest periods (2 to 5 minutes) between sets. A common mistake is to rush through sets. Doing so slows recovery, which in turn compromises your ability to exert maximum effort in succeeding sets.

If Your Goal Is a Combination of Strength and Hypertrophy

If strength and hypertrophy are your goals, design your program around heavier loads that will limit you to 6 to 12 reps (approximately 85 to 70 percent of 1RM) for the core exercises, and 8 to 12 reps in other exercises. Perform 3 to 6 sets in the core exercises and 3 sets in noncore exercises. Rest approximately 1 to 2 minutes between sets.

If Your Goal Is General Muscle Toning

Follow the guidelines presented for muscular endurance programs to accomplish general muscle toning.

If Your Goal Is Body Composition (Reproportioning)

If reproportioning your body is your goal, it is likely that you believe you are carrying too much fat, not enough muscle, or both. Consider doing three things: (a) use a hypertrophy program to increase muscle mass; (b) select your foods more carefully; and (c) begin an aerobic program to increase the number of calories you burn. The texts by Corbin and Lindsey (1997) and Hoeger (1995) provide good direction on how to design aerobic training programs. For the hypertrophy program, simply follow the guidelines presented in this text. When selecting foods, make sure that you eat a balanced diet, increase your intake of complex carbohydrates, and decrease your intake of fats. Also realize that a normal diet will supply the amount of protein typically needed. For more information on nutrition, refer to the text by Clark (1997).

If You Have Other Goals

If you have special needs such as improving athletic performance, or you have a desire to compete in weightlifting or power lifting events, refer to the texts by Baechle (1994), Fleck and Kraemer (1997), and Komi (1992), Baechle and Conroy (1990), and Kraemer and Baechle (1989), and journals published by the National Strength and Conditioning Association. If your interest is bodybuilding consult the text by Sprague (1996). The text by Westcott and Baechle (1998) will be helpful for those interested in programs designed specifically for older populations, and the text by Baechle and Earle (1995) is excellent if you are looking for sample programs for body shaping, muscle toning, strength, or cross-training programs.

2. Select Exercises

The exercises included in your present program are few in number, but they work most of the major muscle areas of the body. It is a basic program that will benefit from the addition of exercises for the lower back, forearm, and calf muscle areas. If your goal is to increase your muscular endurance, muscle size, or strength in a particular body part, it is a good idea to add another exercise designed to work that body part. If you decide to add exercises, do not select more than two per muscle area at this time, and try to not include more than 12 exercises if you are following a 3-days-a-week program. As you will remember from Step 10, the 4-days-a-week program provides a better opportunity to add more exercises. Thus, you may choose to include three exercises for a particular body part if you decide to follow a 4-days-a-week program. When selecting exercises, keep in mind the amount of time you have for training and the number of days in a week you plan to train.

In Table 12.1, decide which of the following muscle areas you want exercises for or want to emphasize (meaning you already have one exercise for this muscle area, and you want to add more). Before completing this task, you may want to refer back to Steps 3 through 8 and Appendix A to review explanations for the various free weight and machine exercises. Remember to consider equipment and spotter requirements. After considering your goals, write in the name of the exercise(s) you want to include to the right of the appropriate muscle areas in Table 12.1.

3. Decide on Frequency of Training

Decide whether you are going to use a 3-days-a-week or 4-days-a-week split program now. If your choice is to use a split program, determine how you will split the exercises among the 4 days. Your decision

Table 12.1	Exercise Selection		
Days	Muscle area	Exercises	
( )	Total body	_____	_____
( )	Chest	_____	_____
( )	Back (upper)	_____	_____
( )	Back (lower)	_____	_____
( )	Shoulders	_____	_____
( )	Arms (back of)	_____	_____
( )	Arms (front of)	_____	_____
( )	Forearm (palm side)	_____	_____
( )	Forearm (knuckle side)	_____	_____
( )	Legs (upper)	_____	_____
( )	Calves	_____	_____
( )	Abdomen	_____	_____

here may require you to reconsider the number of exercises you have selected. Remember, you can include more exercises in split programs than in a 3-days-a-week program. Decide and check which schedule of training you will follow.

( ) 3 days a week—if you checked this option, skip to task #4 and check which approach you will use

( ) 4 days a week (split program)

If you plan to follow a split program, decide and check which of the following you will use:

( ) Chest, shoulders, and arms 2 days; legs and back the other 2 days

( ) Upper body 2 days; lower body 2 days

Once you've made these decisions, write in the parentheses to the left of each muscle area under the "Days" column in Table 12.1 which days you plan to perform the exercises. Use the letters M, T, Th, and F (as shown in Figure 12.1) to do this.

4. Arrange Exercises in the Workout

Next decide on how you will arrange these exercises within a workout. As you recall from Step 10, there are several options. Check which of these arrangements you plan to use:

( ) Larger muscle group exercises first
( ) Alternate push with pull exercises

Now look again (see Table 12.1) at the exercises that you decided to include in your program. Decide how you will arrange the order in which you will perform them. List your order in Table 12.2, using the left-hand column if you plan to follow a 3-days-a-week program and the right-hand column for a 4-day split program.

Now, record the exercises and their order from Table 12.2 onto either Table 12.3, if you checked the 3-days-a-week program, or Table 12.4, if you checked the 4-days-a-week program. The 4-days-a-week chart assumes that you are training Monday/Thursday and Tuesday/Friday.

5. Decide Which Loads to Use

Consider the overload principle and specificity concept in making decisions for assigning the loads needed to achieve the previously stated goals for training.

Select Your Approach

Decide and check which approach to the assignment of loads you will use.

( ) Pyramid
( ) Same load

Table 12.1 Exercise Selection		
Days	Muscle area	Exercises
(T,F)	Total body	*Hang clean*
(M,Th)	Chest	*Bench press* *Dumbbell fly*
(T,F)	Back (upper)	*Bent over row*
(T,F)	Back (lower)	*Back extension*
(M,Th)	Shoulders	*Upright row* *Seated press*
(M,Th)	Arms (back of)	*Triceps extension*
(M,Th)	Arms (front of)	*Biceps curl* *Concentration curl*
(M,Th)	Forearm (palm side)	*Wrist flexion*
(M,Th)	Forearm (knuckle side)	*Wrist extension*
(T,F)	Legs (upper)	*Back squat*
(T,F)	Calves	*Heel raise*
(ALL)	Abdomen	*Bent-knee sit-up*

Figure 12.1 This is an example of a split program where chest, shoulders, and arms are worked on Mondays and Thursdays, back and legs on Tuesdays and Fridays, and abdomen on all workout days.

Table 12.2 Exercise Arrangement			
3 Days/week program		**4 Days/week split program**	
Order	Exercise	Order	Exercise
1.		1.	
2.		2.	
3.		3.	
4.		4.	
5.		5.	
6.		6.	
7.		7.	
8.		8.	
9.		9.	
10.		10.	
11.		11.	
12.		12.	
		13.	
		14.	

Table 12.3 Weight Training Workout Chart (3-Days-a-Week Program)

Name _____

Week # _____

Order	Muscle area	Exercise	Training load	Set	Day 1					Day 2					Day 3				
					1	2	3	4	5	1	2	3	4	5	1	2	3	4	5
1				Wt.															
				Reps															
2				Wt.															
				Reps															
3				Wt.															
				Reps															
4				Wt.															
				Reps															
5				Wt.															
				Reps															
6				Wt.															
				Reps															
7				Wt.															
				Reps															
8				Wt.															
				Reps															
9				Wt.															
				Reps															
10				Wt.															
				Reps															
11				Wt.															
				Reps															
12				Wt.															
				Reps															

Body weight _____

Date _____

Comments _____

Table 12.4 Weight Training Workout Chart (4-Days-a-Week Program)

Name _____

Week #

Order	Monday/Thursday Exercises	Train-ing load	Set	Day 1—Monday 1	2	3	4	5	Day 2—Tuesday 1	2	3	4	5	Day 3—Thursday 1	2	3	4	5	Day 4—Friday 1	2	3	4	5
1			Wt. Reps																				
2			Wt. Reps																				
3			Wt. Reps																				
4			Wt. Reps																				
5			Wt. Reps																				
6			Wt. Reps																				
7			Wt. Reps																				
	Tuesday/Friday Exercises																						
8			Wt. Reps																				
9			Wt. Reps																				
10			Wt. Reps																				
11			Wt. Reps																				
12			Wt. Reps																				
13			Wt. Reps																				
14			Wt. Reps																				
	Body weight																						
	Date																						
	Comments																						

Determine Starting Loads

Using the guidelines given in Step 10 for core and noncore exercises, calculate the loads for the exercises selected. To save time, remember you can use the shortcut method of determining training loads. Record these loads onto either Table 12.3 (3-days-a-week program) or 12.4 (4-days-a-week program) Workout Charts. Do this now.

6. Decide How Many Reps to Perform

Decide and check the number of reps you intend to perform in each set.

( ) 12 to 20
( ) 8 to 12
( ) 1 to 8 core, 8 to 12 noncore
( ) Other (describe)

7. Decide How Many Sets of Each Exercise to Perform

Decide on the number of sets you plan to perform in the exercises listed on your workout chart. Under the heading "Exercise" and just below the name of each exercise, record the sets and reps (indicated previously) you plan to perform (see Figure 12.2). Do this now.

If the number of sets in the core exercises and other exercises are to increase, decide when and in what exercises. Do this now if this is what you plan to do, and remember to apply the cycling concepts discussed in this step.

Core Exercises

The number of sets will increase to ___ after ___ weeks of training in the following core exercises:

Exercise name	Number of sets
_____	_____
_____	_____
_____	_____
_____	_____
_____	_____

Other Exercises (Noncore)

The number of sets will increase to ___ after ___ weeks of training in the following noncore exercises described as:

Exercise name	Number of sets
_____	_____
_____	_____
_____	_____
_____	_____

8. Decide on Length of Rest Periods

Based upon your goals for training, decide on and check which rest period you will use.

( ) 20 to 30 seconds
( ) 30 to 90 seconds
( ) 2 minutes or longer

9. Decide How to Vary the Program

Decide and check which method of varying load intensities you will use.

( ) Within week (e.g., H, L, MH)
( ) Between weeks
( ) Both

Decide and check which method of scheduling load increases you will use.

( ) Weekly
( ) Every 2 weeks
( ) Other (describe)

Determine and check the basis for the scheduled load increases you plan to use.

( ) Increase loads by a specified percentage. How much? ___%
( ) Base decisions on testing, as described in Step 11.

Decide and check the number of training weeks that you will follow before a week of low-intensity training is scheduled.

( ) 5 weeks
( ) 6 weeks
( ) 7 weeks
( ) 8 weeks

Order	Muscle area	Exercise	Training load	Set	Day 1 1	Day 1 2	Day 1 3	Day 2 1	Day 2 2	Day 2 3

Weight Training Workout Chart

Name _Tom Brown_

Week # ____

Order	Muscle area	Exercise	Training load	Set	Wt./Reps	Day 1 (1)	Day 1 (2)	Day 1 (3)	Day 2 (1)	Day 2 (2)	Day 2 (3)
1	Chest	Dumbbell fly 5 x 8-12		Wt.							
				Reps							
2	Back	Biceps curl 3 x 12		Wt.							
				Reps							
3	Shoulder	Standing press 5 x 8-12		Wt.							
				Reps							
4	Arms (front of)	Bent over row 3 x 12		Wt.							
				Reps							
5	Arms (back of)	Triceps extension 3 x 12		Wt.							
				Reps							
6	Legs	Wrist flexion 2 x 12		Wt.							
				Reps							
7	Abdomen	Wrist extension 2 x 12		Wt.							
				Reps							
8		Back squat 5 x 8-12		Wt.							
				Reps							
9		Trunk curl 3 x 20		Wt.							
				Reps							
10				Wt.							
				Reps							
11				Wt.							
				Reps							
12				Wt.							
				Reps							
	Body weight										
	Date										
	Comments										

5 sets of 8 to 12 reps ⟶ (pointing to "5 x 8-12" in Chest row)

Figure 12.2 Workout chart with numbers of sets and reps filled in.

PROGRAM VARIATION

DRILLS

1. Design a 7-Week Program

Depending on which method of program variation you plan to follow, fill in the loads, reps, and sets for all exercises for a 7-week period on a separate sheet of paper. Refer back to Step 11 if you need help.

Success Goal = A 7-week program is developed ___

Success Check
- Overload principle is applied ___
- Specificity concept is applied ___
- Cycling concept is applied ___

2. Modify Your Program Design

Sometimes you will need to modify your program because of injury or a layoff resulting from illness. This drill will prompt you to consider how you can modify your program to accommodate these situations.

Scenario 1: Exercise Selection Modification

After you complain of pain during elbow extension, your doctor recommends that you stop performing all weight training exercises that involve elbow extension (such as the bench press or shoulder press).

Success Goal =
a. List 1 exercise for chest development that does not involve elbow extension ___
b. List 1 exercise for shoulder development that does not involve elbow extension ___

Scenario 2: Exercise Intensity Modification

You have had the flu for the past two weeks and now finally feel good enough to begin training again. Prior to being sick, you had been doing 3 sets of 12-15 reps in 7 exercises.

Success Goal = List the number of sets and reps you will perform on your first day back:
a. Number of sets of each exercise ___
b. Number of reps in each set ___

Scenario 1 Recommendation

Exercises for the chest that do not involve elbow extension include the dumbbell fly (FW shown in Figure A.1 on page 156) and pec deck (C shown in figure 3.2 on page 54). Exercises for the shoulders that do not involve elbow extension include standing lateral raise (FW) (see Figure 12.3 a and b) and lateral raise (M) (see Figure 12.4 a and b).

Scenario 2 Recommendation

Missing training sessions for a week or more should prompt you to reduce the intensity of training in your first week back, as the detraining that occurs during a layoff will lower your strength and endurance. A sensible approach is to begin with one set of each exercise. Keep the reps the same and allow yourself at least an extra minute of rest between sets. Follow these guidelines for the first week back and then resume your original program unless you still feel run down at the beginning of the second week back.

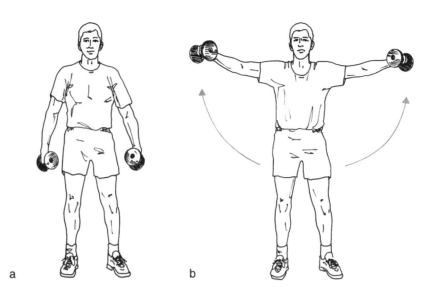

Figure 12.3 The standing lateral raise (FW for shoulder development) does not involve elbow extension..

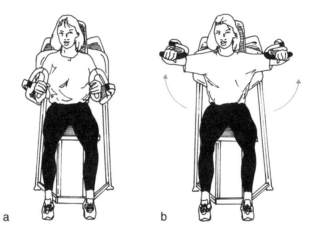

Figure 12.4 The lateral raise (M for shoulder development) does not involve elbow extension.

YOUR PERSONALIZED PROGRAM SUCCESS SUMMARY

The activities included in this step require an application of all that you have learned concerning how to design a weight training program. You are now capable not only of designing a program that meets your present needs, but you might also want to look ahead and consider how to modify or manipulate the program design variables during the next year. Individuals who are very serious about training usually develop short training cycles that are a part of larger cycles, which in turn are a part of even larger yearly cycles. It may be too early for you to be concerned about such detailed planning. In the future, however, you are encouraged to review the resources cited in Steps 10 and 11. Also consider adding a total body exercise such as the power clean presented in Appendix A.

In the process of learning about equipment, exercise techniques, and program design variables, you have probably gained a better appreciation of the expertise required to design programs for athletes in various sports, and programs for special populations (prepubescents, seniors, cardiacs, arthritics, and those with osteoporosis, hypertension, or injuries). It is again appropriate to emphasize here that no program will amount to much unless it is approached with a positive attitude. If you train hard, train smart, and eat sensibly, you are virtually guaranteed success and the opportunity to enjoy "wearing your workouts" proudly.

RATING YOUR PROGRESS

Each exercise you completed in this book had Success Goals and Success Checks associated with it that were designed to prompt you to develop your physical skills and knowledge. The following inventory allows you to rate the overall progress you have made. Read the items carefully and respond to them thoughtfully.

5 = Excellent 4 = Above average 3 = Average 2 = Below average 1 = Unsuccessful

Technique and Skill

Rate your success level in correctly performing exercises for the following muscle groups.

1. Chest ___
2. Back ___
3. Shoulders ___

4. Arms ___
5. Legs ___
6. Abdomen ___

Anatomical Knowledge

Rate your knowledge of the names of specific muscles in each of the following muscle groups.

1. Chest ___
2. Back ___
3. Shoulders ___

4. Arms ___
5. Legs ___
6. Abdomen ___

Program Design Concepts

Rate your level of knowledge and understanding of the following program design variables.

1. Selecting exercises ___
2. Training frequency ___
3. Arranging exercises ___
4. Selecting loads ___
5. Number of reps ___

6. Number of sets ___
7. Length of rest periods ___
8. Varying intensity ___
9. Designing a comprehensive weight training program ___

Outcomes of Training

Rate the progress you have made in the following areas.

1. Strength ___
2. Muscular size ___
3. Muscular endurance ___

4. Flexibility ___
5. Body composition ___

Appearance, Attitude, and Self-Concept

Rate the impact of training on the following areas.

1. Appearance ___
2. Attitude ___
3. Self-concept ___

APPENDIX A: ALTERNATIVE EXERCISES

This section includes one or more exercises for each muscle group presented in the basic program, plus exercises for the forearm, calf, and lower back and two total body exercises. These exercises can be used to complement or replace exercises currently included in your program. When more than one exercise is presented for the same muscle group, you might wonder which is best. That depends on the preference of each individual: what is best for one is not necessarily best for another. The exercises presented in Steps 3 through 8 are what we consider the best based on our knowledge and experience. However, you should experiment with a variety of exercises and decide for yourself which are best for your program.

A priority should be given to adding exercises for the forearm, calf, and lower back and one total body exercise because they are needed to provide a balanced program. Each of the exercises, except the total body exercises, in this section is identified as a "push" or "pull" exercise to assist you in arranging them in your workout. Also note that in Steps 3 through 8 you were referred to the anatomical drawings in Appendix B along with the Keys to Success. This made it easy for you to associate exercises with the muscles they work. Also, try to remember the locations of the specific muscles mentioned in each of the following exercise descriptions.

Exercises in this section are grouped and organized in the following order:

1. Chest: Dumbbell fly
2. Upper back: Lat pull-down
3. Lower back: Back extension exercise
4. Shoulders: Upright row
5. Upper arms: Concentration curl and supine triceps extension
6. Forearms: Wrist flexion and extension
7. Upper legs: Back squat, knee extension, and knee flexion
8. Lower legs (calves): Heel raises
9. Abdomen: Bent-knee sit-up
10. Total body exercises: Deadlift, high pull, and hang clean

Determining Loads for Newly Added Exercises

Now that you have gained some experience in selecting and using loads, follow these procedures for establishing loads for these new exercises:

1. Begin learning new exercises using an empty bar or the lightest weight plate possible, and perform 15 reps.
2. Next make a guess at the poundage that will allow you to perform 12 to 15 reps, and perform only 6 reps with it.
3. After approximately 2 minutes, increase the load by 10 pounds and perform as many reps as possible. Add 20 pounds for the total body exercises.
4. Next refer to Step 11 for the shortcut for determining training loads.

5. If after using the training load you find the reps performed are not in accord with your goals for training, use one of the Load Adjustment Charts in Steps 3 through 8 (see practice procedure 5).

Consider Other Exercises

The exercises in this and in previous sections of this book are but a few of the beneficial weight training exercises from which you can choose. There are many more that are illustrated and/or explained in the text listed in the reference section of this book. In addition to the standard exercises that are performed using free weights and machines, there are also those that involve the use of thin bands of elastic, elastic tubing, weighted batons, and hand weights. Often these are ideal options for resistance training that are economical and require little space to perform. For ideas on how to use this type of quipment refer to the text by Westcott and Baechle (1998).

Concentrate on Using Proper Technique

During your warm-up and training sets, concentrate on and use the proper grip, body position, movement pattern, breathing, and range of motion, along with controlled speed and smooth execution. Ask a partner to check off the Keys to Success items as you demonstrate them. Also, take time to visualize the techniques of a new exercise before performing them.

Alternative Exercise for Developing the Chest

The dumbbell fly exercise (see Figure A.1) is frequently used as a supplement or alternative exercise for the chest exercises presented in Step 3. The major area involved is the same (pectoralis major). This is a pushing exercise. Watch out for these common errors:

1. Attempting to use too much weight
2. Flexing the elbows too much

FIGURE A.1 **KEYS TO SUCCESS**

DUMBBELL FLY
Preparation Phase

1. Grip with palms facing inward ___
2. Torso lying on bench with head, shoulders, and buttocks in contact ___
3. Legs flexed 90 degrees ___
4. Feet flat on floor ___
5. Arms slightly flexed at elbow ___

a

Downward Execution Phase

1. Slowly lower dumbbells, keeping elbows perpendicular to torso ___
2. Lower dumbbells to chest height ___
3. Keep elbows slightly flexed ___
4. Do not twist or arch body ___
5. Inhale while lowering ___

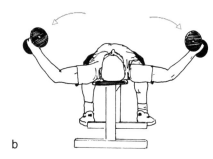

b

Upward Execution Phase

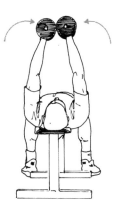

1. Slowly return dumbbells to starting position ___
2. Keep feet flat on floor ___
3. Keep head, shoulders, and buttocks on the bench ___
4. Exhale during return ___

c

Alternative Exercise for Developing the Upper Back

The lat pull-down (see Figure A.2) develops the upper back (latissimus dorsi, rhomboids, trapezius) and involves some chest (pectorals), and anterior upper arm (biceps) muscles. This exercise is considered to be an alternative exercise for the back exercises presented in Step 4 and is a pulling exercise. Be careful to avoid the following common errors:

1. Using the torso to complete the movement
2. Allowing the weight stack to drop quickly back to the starting position

FIGURE A.2 **KEYS TO SUCCESS**

LAT PULL-DOWN

a

b

c

Preparation Phase

1. Grip overhand, slightly wider than shoulder width ___
2. Assume a kneeling or seated position ___
3. Torso tilted slightly backward ___
4. Arms extended ___

Downward Execution Phase

1. Pull straight down in front of face ___
2. Pull smoothly, keeping elbows out and away from body ___
3. Pull bar past chin until it touches upper chest ___
4. Exhale as bar touches chest ___

Upward Execution Phase

1. Extend arms slowly upward ___
2. Do not allow weight plate to hit weight stack ___
3. Fully extend arms ___
4. Inhale while extending arms ___

Alternative Exercises for Developing the Lower Back

The back extension exercise is used to strengthen the muscles of the lower back (erector spinae and quadratus lumborum). This exercise (see Figure A.3) is performed on the back extension station of a multi- or single-unit machine. Watch out for the following common errors:

1. Hyperextending in the up position
2. Allowing the torso to drop quickly back to the head-pointed-down position

FIGURE A.3   **KEYS TO SUCCESS**

BACK EXTENSION
Preparation Phase

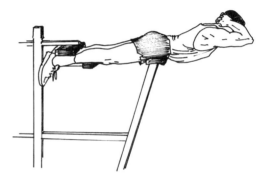

1. Hips on front pad, heels under rear pad ___
2. Torso rigid, horizontal, facing down ___
3. Hands folded behind head ___

a

Downward Execution Phase

1. Slowly lower torso to head-pointed-down position ___
2. Inhale while lowering ___

b

Upward Execution Phase

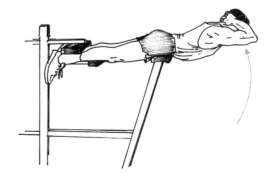

1. Slowly raise torso to horizontal position ___
2. Do not hyperextend ___
3. Do not thrust arms ___
4. Exhale when nearing horizontal position ___

c

Alternative Exercise for Developing the Shoulders

The upright row (see Figure A.4) develops the shoulders (deltoids) and is considered to be an alternative exercise for the overhead pressing exercises presented in Step 5. This exercise can be performed using a barbell, dumbbells, or the low pulley station on a multi- or single-unit machine. It is a pulling exercise. Watch out for the following common errors:

1. Allowing the elbows to drop below the wrists
2. Allowing the bar to drop quickly back to the down position

FIGURE A.4 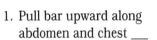 **KEYS TO SUCCESS**

UPRIGHT ROW

Preparation Phase

1. Grip overhand, hands 2 to 4 inches apart ___
2. Torso erect ___
3. Feet shoulder-width apart ___
4. Arms straight ___
5. Bar rests on thighs ___

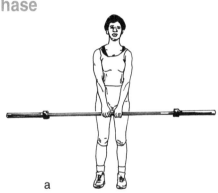

a

Upward Execution Phase

1. Pull bar upward along abdomen and chest ___
2. Elbows pointed outward ___
3. Elbows higher than wrists ___
4. Pull until elbows reach shoulder height ___
5. Exhale as bar nears shoulders ___
6. Pause briefly at top position ___

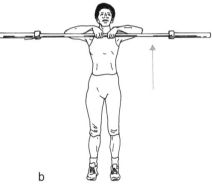

b

Downward Execution Phase

1. Inhale as the bar starts downward ___
2. Lower bar slowly and smoothly ___
3. Pause at bottom ___

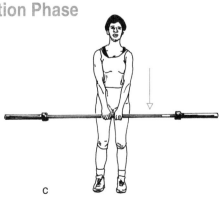

c

Alternative Exercise for Developing the Anterior Upper Arm

The concentration curl (see Figure A.5) is frequently used as a supplement to other biceps exercises presented in Step 6, often to add definition to, or to "peak out," the biceps. This pulling exercise is performed using a dumbbell. Watch out for the following common errors:

1. Leaning back as the dumbbell is curled toward the chin
2. Allowing the dumbbell to drop quickly back to the starting position

FIGURE A.5 | **KEYS TO SUCCESS**

CONCENTRATION CURL

Preparation Phase

1. Seated on bench, upper torso leaning forward ___
2. Feet wider than shoulder-width apart, flat on floor ___
3. Grip underhand ___
4. Arm straight, upper arm braced against your leg ___

a

Upward Execution Phase

1. Slowly curl dumbbell toward chin ___
2. Maintain stable forward lean position ___
3. Pause at full flexion ___
4. Exhale as dumbbell nears your chin ___

b

Downward Execution Phase

1. Slowly lower dumbbell to starting position ___
2. Maintain forward lean position ___
3. Inhale while lowering ___

c

Alternative Exercise for Developing the Posterior Upper Arm

The supine triceps extension (see Figure A.6) can be used as an alternative to the triceps (posterior upper arm) exercises presented in Step 6. This pushing exercise is performed lying on a bench using a barbell or dumbbell. Watch out for the following common errors:

1. Outward and foreward movement of the upper arms
2. Elbows not perpendicular at the start of each rep

FIGURE A.6

KEYS TO SUCCESS

SUPINE TRICEPS EXTENSION

Preparation Phase

Spotting Keys

1. Stand at partner's head ___
2. Hand bar to partner ___

a

Exercise Keys

1. Grip overhand, hands evenly spaced 8 inches apart ___
2. Stable position flat on bench ___
3. Legs flexed 90 degrees ___
4. Feet flat on floor ___
5. Elbows point straight upward ___

Downward Execution Phase

Spotting Keys

1. Keep hands under bar to protect partner's head ___
2. Help control downward speed of bar ___

b

Exercise Keys

1. Keep upper arms stationary ___
2. Keep elbows straight up ___
3. Do not allow elbows to bow out ___
4. Slowly lower bar ___
5. Inhale while lowering ___

Upward Execution Phase

Spotting Keys

1. Assist partner through sticking point if needed ___
2. Take weight after last repetition and return to floor ___

c

Exercise Keys

1. Push upward to extend the elbows ___
2. Keep elbows pointed straight up ___
3. Keep elbows from bowing out ___
4. Exhale when nearing top position ___

Alternative Exercise for Developing the Forearm

Wrist flexion (palms up) and wrist extension (palms down) exercises performed on a bench are common exercises for developing the lower arm (forearm). These exercises can be performed using a barbell (see Figure A.7), dumbbells, or the low pulley station on a multi- or single-unit machine. Watch out for the following common errors:

1. Using elbow flexion to begin or complete movement
2. Lifting the buttocks off the bench

FIGURE A.7   **KEYS TO SUCCESS**

WRIST FLEXION AND EXTENSION

Preparation Phase

1. Grip underhand (flexion) or overhand (extension), hands close together ___
2. Forearms supported by bench, wrists over edge ___
3. Torso seated on bench, leaning forward ___

a

Downward Execution Phase

1. Slowly lower bar over edge of bench ___
2. Keep buttocks on bench ___
3. Keep elbows on bench ___
4. Inhale while lowering ___

b

Upward Execution Phase

1. Slowly return wrists to starting position ___
2. Do not use elbow flexion ___
3. Keep body still ___
4. Exhale during upward movement ___

c

Alternative Exercises for Developing the Upper Legs

The back squat (see Figure A.8), a popular exercise among athletes and body builders, is an excellent total body functional exercise that also teaches individuals how to properly squat down without unduly stressing the knees and lower back. It develops the lower back (erector spinae), hips (gluteal muscles), front of upper leg (quadriceps), and back of the upper leg (hamstrings). Watch out for the following common errors:

1. Bar positioned too high on the neck
2. Feet too close together
3. Lowering the head to look at the floor
4. Allowing the knees to move forward in front of the feet
5. Leaning forward to rack the bar

Caution: The back squat exercise should never be performed without a spotter. When only one spotter is available, this exercise should be performed in a rack similar to that shown in Figure A.8.

FIGURE
A.8   **KEYS TO SUCCESS**

BACK SQUAT
Preparation Phase

Spotting Keys

1. Stand directly behind and close to your partner ___
2. Place your hands close to bar ___
3. Keep your back flat and knees slightly flexed ___
4. Assist only if necessary ___

a

Exercise Keys

1. Overhand grip, slightly wider than shoulder width ___
2. Bar positioned on shoulders at base of neck ___
3. Torso−hips directly under bar, chest out, shoulders back, head up ___
4. Feet flat on floor slightly wider than shoulder width ___

Downward Execution Phase

Spotting Keys

1. Squat with partner ___
2. Track bar with hands ___

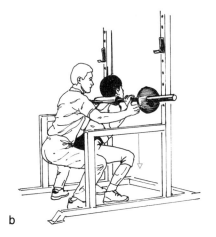

b

Exercise Keys

1. Squat down slowly ___
2. Avoid excessive forward lean ___
3. Feet flat on floor with knees in line with the feet ___
4. Continue squatting until bottoms of thighs are parallel to the floor ___
5. Inhale on descent ___

Upward Execution Phase

Spotting Keys

1. Ascend with partner ___
2. Keep hands close to bar ___
3. Assist only when necessary ___

c

Exercise Keys

1. Begin movement with legs first ___
2. Keep head up and chest out ___
3. Straighten hips and knees ___
4. Exhale during sticking point ___

Racking the Bar

Spotting Keys

1. Walk with partner until bar is racked ___
2. Tell your partner when the bar is safely racked ___

d

Exercise Keys

1. Walk forward until bar contacts rack ___
2. Squat down until bar is in the rack ___
3. Never lean forward to rack bar ___

Two additional exercises, knee extension (see Figure A.9) and knee flexion (see Figure A.10) develop the quadriceps and hamstrings, respectively. These exercises can be used as alternates for the lunge and leg press exercises presented in Step 7. Watch out for the following common errors in the knee extension exercise:

1. Lifting the buttocks off the bench
2. Allowing the weight to drop quickly back to the starting position

KEYS TO SUCCESS

KNEE EXTENSION
Preparation Phase

1. Assume a sitting position ___
2. Grip edge of table, chair, or handles ___
3. Torso erect, lower back flat ___
4. Head up, facing forward ___
5. Shins and ankles behind pads ___

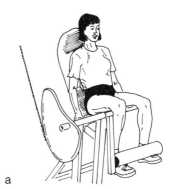

a

Upward Execution Phase

1. Slowly extend lower leg through a complete range of motion ___
2. Exhale while extending ___
3. Pause briefly in extended position ___

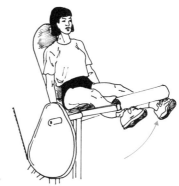

b

Downward Execution Phase

1. Slowly lower weight ___
2. Keep buttocks in contact with seat ___
3. Pause at bottom position ___
4. Do not allow weight plate to hit weight stack ___
5. Inhale while lowering weight ___

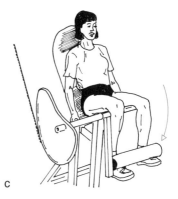

c

The knee flexion exercise for the hamstrings is often neglected in favor of the knee extension for the quadriceps, which are more visible and easier to develop. However, you should include the same number of sets for both. Watch out for the following common errors:

1. Allowing the hips or chest to rise off the bench
2. Allowing weight to drop quickly back to the starting position

FIGURE A.10 **KEYS TO SUCCESS**

KNEE FLEXION
Preparation Phase

1. Assume a prone position ___
2. Grip handles or edge of bench ___
3. Hips flat, chest on bench ___
4. Kneecaps below edge of bench, ankles under pads ___

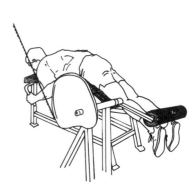

a

Upward Execution Phase

1. Flex heels as far as possible toward buttocks ___
2. Exhale during upward movement ___
3. Pause briefly in fully flexed position ___

b

Downward Execution Phase

1. Lower weight slowly ___
2. Do not allow hips to rise off bench ___
3. Keep chest on bench ___
4. Inhale during downward movement ___

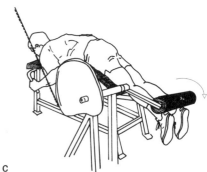

c

Alternative Exercise for Developing the Lower Leg (Calves)

Heel raises, or plantar flexion at the ankle joint, exercise the calf muscles (soleus, gastrocnemius). This exercise can be performed using a barbell across the shoulders, holding dumbbells (see Figure A.11), or using the overhead press station on a single- or multi-unit machine. Be sure that the board being used is stable. Watch out for the following common errors:

1. Allowing the knees to flex and extend during movement
2. Not lowering heels to full stretch

FIGURE
A.11 **KEYS TO SUCCESS**

HEEL RAISE
Preparation Phase

1. Place bar on shoulders, or hold dumbbells ___
2. Use elevated, stable surface approximately 6 inches high ___
3. Place feet hip-width apart ___
4. Place the balls of both feet near the edge ___
5. Vary feet from straight ahead to slightly outward to inward ___
6. Keep torso erect and knees straight ___

a

Upward Execution Phase

1. Slowly raise heels as high as possible ___
2. Pause momentarily before lowering ___
3. Allow only calves to do the work ___
4. Exhale as you ascend ___

b

Downward Execution Phase

1. Slowly lower heels to full stretch without pain ___
2. Do not move torso or flex knees ___
3. Inhale as you descend ___

c

Alternative Exercise for Developing the Abdominals

The bent-knee sit-up (see Figure A.12) can be performed either on a flat surface or on an incline board. Begin performing this exercise on a flat surface. The bent-knee sit-up is completed when the shoulders are elevated 30 degrees and then returned to the starting position. This exercise is a supplement or an alternative to the twisting trunk curl and the machine curl presented in Step 8. Watch out for the following common errors:

1. Raising the upper torso past 30 degrees
2. Bouncing at the bottom of the movement

FIGURE A.12 **KEYS TO SUCCESS**

BENT-KNEE SIT-UP
Preparation Phase

1. Back flat on floor ___
2. Knees flexed at 110 degrees ___
3. Feet flat on floor ___
4. Arms folded across chest ___

a

Forward Execution Phase

1. Curl chin to chest first ___
2. Raise shoulders and upper back to 30 degrees ___
3. Pause in this position ___
4. Exhale during upward phase ___

b

Backward Execution Phase

1. Slowly return to starting position ___
2. Keep chin to chest until shoulders touch ___
3. Lower head to mat ___
4. Pause, do not bounce, at bottom ___
5. Inhale during downward phase ___

c

Total Body Exercise Options

The deadlift, high pull, and hang clean exercises are especially popular with athletic teams whose activities require total body strength/power and explosive movements. They are also ideal for those who want to develop muscular bulk in the large muscles of the legs, hips, and lower and upper back. All three exercises are free weight exercises and require a designated area. The designated area for these exercises should be separate from the rest of the lifting area for safety reasons and should have some protection for the floor in the event that the bar is allowed to drop quickly. A spotter should not be used in these exercises because if something goes wrong during the movement you can drop the bar without injury. Also, a spotter attempting to catch the bar during one of these exercises can easily be injured or could possibly cause injury to you.

Deadlift

The deadlift (see Figure A.13), usually considered a power lifting exercise, is a total body functional exercise that not only develops strength in almost all major muscles and muscle groups, but teaches how to properly lift an object from the floor such as a barbell or a child. Body builders also use this exercise and a modification of it (straight-leg deadlift) to develop the musculature of both the upper and lower back, hips, and upper legs. The straight-leg deadlift with locked knees is not recommended because it causes excessive strain on the lower back, and the same results can be obtained by doing the bent-leg deadlift correctly.

Approach the bar until your shins touch it, with your feet less than shoulder-width apart and your toes pointed slightly outward. Use the markings on the bar to ensure that your feet are equidistant from the weight plates. Use an alternate grip with your hands equally spaced just outside your legs. Squat down with your shins still touching the bar; keep your arms straight, shoulders pulled back, head up, and eyes looking forward. Start the movement by lifting with the legs; keep the bar brushing against your legs during the entire movement. Your hips should stay low and begin to push forward as soon as the bar passes your knees. Your back should remain flat throughout the exercise. Continue lifting until your knees and hips are straight and your shoulders are pulled up and back. To lower the bar to the floor, start by flexing at the hips until the bar passes your knees, then use your legs to lower the weight to the starting position. Inhale as you start the lift and exhale after passing the sticking point.

KEYS TO SUCCESS

DEADLIFT

a

b

c

Preparation Phase

1. Place your shins against the bar less than shoulder-width apart ___
2. Toes pointed slightly outward ___
3. Alternate grip slightly wider than shoulder width ___
4. Hips low, shoulders high and pulled back, arms straight ___
5. Head up with eyes focused straight ahead or higher ___

Upward Execution Phase

1. Inhale before pulling ___
2. Begin to straighten your knees while your hips stay low ___
3. Back remains straight and fully extended ___
4. Arms straight ___
5. Bar stays close to shins and knees ___
6. Bar lightly touches above your knees and slides up your thighs ___
7. Shoulders high and pulled back ___

Finish (Lockout) Phase

1. Knees and hips finish straightening at the same time ___
2. Pull shoulders up and back until they form a straight line with hips and feet ___

Downward Execution Phase

1. Begin to flex at hips and knees ___
2. Keep back straight and shoulders pulled back ___
3. Use legs to complete downward movement to the floor after the bar passes your knees ___
4. Keep bar close to your thighs, knees, and shins throughout the movement ___
5. Keep the bar under control while lowering ___

High Pull

The high pull is started from the midthigh (hang) position (see Figure A.14a). The techniques used to reach the midthigh position are exactly the same as the preparation and execution upward (floor-to-thigh) phases described in Lifting Fundamentals (review Step 1, Figures 1.4 and 1.5). From this position you should explosively jump straight up using knee and hip extension, ankle plantar flexion, and a violent shrugging of the shoulders (see Figure A.14b). Up to this point your arms have functioned like ropes attaching the bar to your shoulders. However, not until the end of this straight upward jump do your arms begin to pull on the bar as your elbows flex and move upward and sideward. Pull the bar as high as possible to your chest (Figure A.14c), then return the weight to the midthigh (hang) position. You should lower the bar to your thighs while flexing your hips and knees. Your back should remain straight, with your shoulders pulled back. Keep the bar close to your chest and abdominal area as you lower the bar to your thighs. Watch out for the following common errors:

1. Failing to completely extend the knees and hips
2. Relying on the arms to accelerate the bar off the thighs

FIGURE A.14

KEYS TO SUCCESS

HIGH PULL

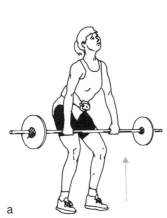

a
Preparation Phase
1. Properly lift bar from floor to thigh ___
2. Keep your arms straight ___
3. Shift balance to ball of foot ___
4. Keep torso rigid, head up, and chest high ___

b
Upward Execution Phase
1. Jump straight up, using knee and hip extension ___
2. Rise as high as possible on your toes, using ankle plantar flexion ___
3. Shrug your shoulders as high as possible ___
4. Pull upward with your arms by flexing elbows ___
5. Elbows should move upward and sideward ___
6. Keep bar close to chest and pull as high as possible ___

c
Downward Execution Phase
1. Keep bar close to your chest and abdominal area ___
2. On the bar's descent, flex your hips and knees ___
3. Keep your back flat or slightly hyperextended ___
4. Keep your shoulders back ___
5. Keep control of the bar as you lower it to midthigh ___

Hang Clean

The hang clean is executed exactly like the high pull except that the bar is caught (racked) on the shoulders after reaching the highest point.

At the highest point of the high pull (see Figure A.15a), you must shift your body rapidly under the bar to catch the weight (see Figure A.15b), while rapidly rotating your elbows down under and then up in front of the bar as it touches your shoulders and clavicle (see Figure A.15c). As your elbows rotate around the bar, you should flex your knees so that the barbell lands on your shoulders. At the same time your knees should act like shock absorbers to smoothly cushion the downward momentum. The weight should never be caught with the knees fully extended, forcing the vertebrae to serve as shock absorbers; this could cause injury to the back. Be sure to catch the weight on your shoulders and clavicle. Watch out for the following common errors:

1. Failing to completely extend the knees and hips

FIGURE A.15 | **KEYS TO SUCCESS**

HANG CLEAN

a

b

c

Preparation Phase

1. Start from the midthigh position ___
2. Lift bar from thigh to shoulder ___
3. Explosively jump and shrug shoulders ___
4. Pull the bar as high as possible ___

Moving Under the Bar

1. Rotate your elbows rapidly under and then up in front of the bar ___
2. Flex your knees to 1/4 squat ___
3. Exhale ___

Racking the Bar

1. Catch the bar on your shoulders and clavicle ___
2. Gradually straighten your knees, assume an erect stance ___
3. Keep your chest high with elbows pointing forward ___
4. Inhale ___

Lowering the Bar

1. Flex your knees and hips ___
2. Keep shoulders back and back flat ___
3. Keep bar close to your chest and abdominal area ___
4. Lower bar with control to midthigh ___

APPENDIX B: MUSCLES OF THE BODY

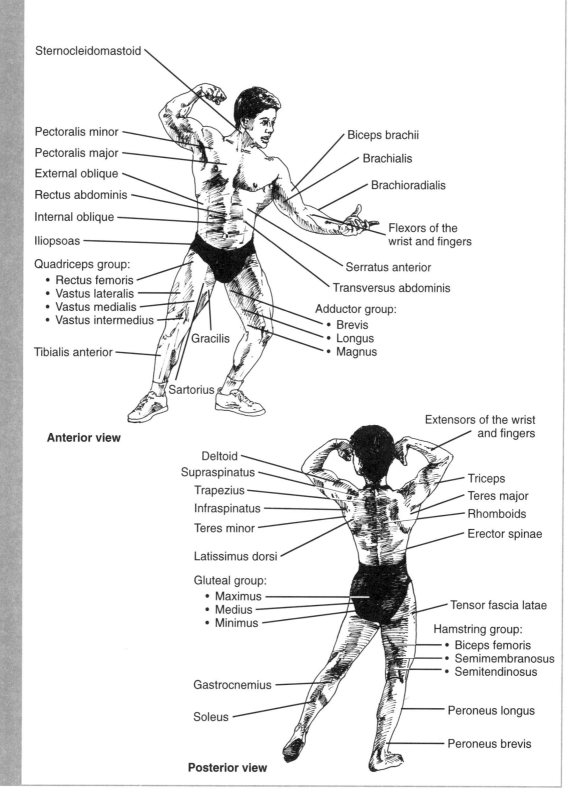

Sternocleidomastoid

Pectoralis minor
Pectoralis major
External oblique
Rectus abdominis
Internal oblique
Iliopsoas
Quadriceps group:
• Rectus femoris
• Vastus lateralis
• Vastus medialis
• Vastus intermedius

Gracilis

Tibialis anterior

Sartorius

Biceps brachii
Brachialis
Brachioradialis
Flexors of the
wrist and fingers
Serratus anterior
Transversus abdominis
Adductor group:
• Brevis
• Longus
• Magnus

Anterior view

Extensors of the wrist
and fingers

Deltoid
Supraspinatus
Trapezius
Infraspinatus
Teres minor
Latissimus dorsi

Gluteal group:
• Maximus
• Medius
• Minimus

Gastrocnemius

Soleus

Triceps
Teres major
Rhomboids
Erector spinae

Tensor fascia latae
Hamstring group:
• Biceps femoris
• Semimembranosus
• Semitendinosus

Peroneus longus

Peroneus brevis

Posterior view

APPENDIX C: WEIGHT TRAINING WORKOUT CHART

The best way to establish a regular training program is to record your workout progress. Make three copies of the following 3-days per week workout chart. Add the week numbers and your name.

Select the appropriate core exercises from Steps 3 through 8, and repeat this basic program for at least 6 weeks before adding more exercises to your program. Be persistent and let no more than 72 hours go by without training in order to avoid any decrease in training status.

Weight Training Workout Chart (3-Days-a-Week Program)

Name _____

Order	Muscle area	Exercise	Train-ing load	Set	Week # ___ Day 1 1	2	3	Week # ___ Day 2 1	2	3	Day 3 1	2	3	Week # ___ Day 1 1	2	3	Day 2 1	2	3	Day 3 1	2	3
1	Chest			Wt.																		
				Reps																		
2	Back			Wt.																		
				Reps																		
3	Shoulder			Wt.																		
				Reps																		
4	Arms (front of)			Wt.																		
				Reps																		
5	Arms (back of)			Wt.																		
				Reps																		
6	Legs			Wt.																		
				Reps																		
7	Abdomen			Wt.																		
				Reps																		
8				Wt.																		
				Reps																		
9				Wt.																		
				Reps																		
10				Wt.																		
				Reps																		
11				Wt.																		
				Reps																		
12				Wt.																		
				Reps																		
Body weight																						
Date																						
Comments																						

APPENDIX D: KILOGRAM CONVERSION TABLE

To convert pounds to kilograms, multiply pounds by .453597. For an estimate use .4536. In this chart numbers are rounded off by reducing to the nearest quarter. An example: 185 pounds multiplied by .453597 equals 83.9154. The kilograms are given here as 83.75 rather than 84.00. To convert kilograms to pounds, multiply kilograms by 2.2046. For a quick estimate use 2.2.

Pounds	Kilograms	Pounds	Kilograms	Kilograms	Pounds	Kilograms	Pounds
2.5	1.00	205	92.75	2.5	5.5	95	209.25
5	2.25	210	95.25	5.0	11.0	97.5	214.75
10	4.50	215	97.50	7.5	16.5	100	220.25
15	6.75	220	99.75	10.0	22.0	102.5	225.75
20	9.00	225	102.00	12.5	27.5	105	231.25
25	11.25	230	104.25	15.0	33.0	107.5	236.75
30	13.50	235	106.50	17.5	38.5	110	242.5
35	15.75	240	108.75	20.0	44.0	112.5	248
40	18.00	245	111.00	22.5	49.5	115	253.5
45	20.25	250	113.25	25	55	117.5	259
50	22.50	255	115.50	27.5	60.5	120	264.5
55	24.75	260	117.75	30	66	122.5	270
60	27.00	265	120.00	32.5	71.5	125	275.5
65	29.25	270	122.25	35	77	127.5	281
70	31.75	275	124.50	37.5	82.5	130	286.5
75	34.00	280	127.00	40	88	132.5	292
80	36.25	285	129.25	42.5	93.5	135	297.5
85	38.50	290	131.50	45	99	137.5	303
90	40.75	295	133.75	47.5	104.5	140	308.5
95	43.00	300	136.00	50	110	142.5	314
100	45.25	305	138.25	52.5	115.5	145	319.5
105	47.50	310	140.50	55	121.25	147.5	325
110	49.75	315	142.75	57.5	126.75	150	330.5
115	52.00	320	145.00	60	132.25	152.5	336
120	54.25	325	147.25	62.5	137.75	155	341.5
125	56.50	330	149.50	65	143.25	157.5	347
130	58.75	335	151.75	67.5	148.75	160	352.5
135	61.00	340	154.00	70	154.25	162.5	358
140	63.50	345	156.25	72.5	159.75	165	363.75
145	65.75	350	158.75	75	165.25	167.5	369.25
150	68.00	355	161.00	77.5	170.75	170	374.75
155	70.25	360	163.25	80	176.25	172.5	380.25
160	72.50	365	165.50	82.5	181.75	175	385.75
165	74.75	370	167.75	85	187.25	177.5	391.25
170	77.00	375	170.00	87.5	192.75	180	396.75
175	79.25	380	172.25	90	198.25	182.5	402.25
180	81.50	385	174.50	92.5	203.75		
185	83.75	390	176.75				
190	86.00	395	179.00				
195	88.25	400	181.25				
200	90.50						

GLOSSARY

absolute strength—A comparative expression of strength based upon actual load lifted.

adipose tissue—Fat tissue.

aerobic—In the presence of oxygen.

aerobic capacity—A measurement of physical fitness based on maximum oxygen uptake.

aerobic energy system—The metabolic pathway that requires oxygen for the production of adenosine triphosphate (ATP).

aerobic exercise—When a person is exercising aerobically, the muscle cells are receiving enough oxygen to continue at a steady state. Walking, biking, running, swimming, and cross-country skiing are examples of this form of exercise.

all-or-none law—A muscle cell that is stimulated by the brain will contract maximally or not at all; a stimulus of insufficient intensity will not elicit a contraction.

alternated grip—A grip in which one hand is supinated and the other hand is pronated. Also called a mixed grip. It is the grip used in the deadlift exercise (Appendix A) and for spotting the bench press (Step 3). Thumbs point in the same direction.

amino acids—Nitrogen-containing compounds that form the building blocks of protein.

anabolic—Tissue building that is conducive to the constructive process of metabolism.

anabolic steroid—Testosterone, or a substance resembling testosterone, which stimulates body growth anabolically as well as androgenically.

anaerobic—In the absence of oxygen.

anaerobic exercise—Exercise during which the energy needed is provided without the utilization of inspired oxygen. Examples include weightlifting and the 100-meter sprint.

androgen—Any compound that has masculinizing properties.

assistance exercises—Exercises that are used as supplementary to the main or core exercises. For example, knee extensions may be used as a supplement to the squat, a core exercise.

atrophy—A decrease in the cross-sectional size of the muscle fiber due to a lack of use or disease or starvation.

barbell—A piece of free weight equipment used in two-arm exercises, it is a long bar on which weight plates may be placed on both ends.

basal metabolic rate (BMR)—The amount of energy, expressed in kilocalories, that the body requires to carry on its normal functions at rest.

bodybuilding—A sport that involves weight training to develop muscle hypertrophy. Bodybuilders are judged on their muscle size, definition, symmetry, and posing skill.

body composition—The quantification of the various components of the body, especially fat and muscle. Various methods exist for its determination; skinfold calipers, girth measurement, impedance, and underwater (hydrostatic) weighing are methods commonly used.

calorie—The measure of the amount of energy released from food or expended in metabolism (exercise). The standard unit is termed a kilocalorie (Kcal or Calorie), or 1,000 calories, but is usually incorrectly expressed by many as simply a "calorie."

carbohydrate (CHO)—A group of chemical compounds composed of carbon, hydrogen, and oxygen. Examples include sugars, starches, and cellulose. It is a basic foodstuff that contains approximately 4 kilocalories per gram.

cardiac muscle—A type of striated (involuntary) muscle tissue located only in the heart.

cardiorespiratory fitness—This category of fitness (cardio—heart, respiratory—lungs) pertains to the efficiency of the heart and lungs to deliver oxygen to the working muscles.

circuit training—A variation of interval training that uses weights and timed work and rest periods. This type of weight training program is typically designed to increase muscular endurance.

closed grip—A grip in which the fingers and the thumbs are wrapped (closed) around the bar.

collars—That component on a barbell or dumbbell that keeps weight plates from sliding toward the hands.

common grip—A grip in which the hands are placed at about shoulder width and equidistant from the weight plates.

compound set—Performing two exercises that work the same muscle group consecutively, without rest between them. For example, a compound set for the chest would be a set of bench presses followed immediately by a set of dumbbell flys. Often this method of training is misnamed a "super set."

concentric muscular action—A type of muscular action characterized by tension being developed followed by the muscle shortening (e.g., the upward phase of a biceps curl).

conditioning—A process of improving the capacity of the body to produce energy and do work.

cool-down—The period in which an individual performs light or mild exercise immediately following the completion of a training session. The primary purpose of a cool-down is to facilitate the movement of blood back to the heart and to enable the body to gradually return to a resting state.

core exercises—The primary weight training exercises that stress the large muscle groups of the body.

cycles—A specific period of time (weeks, months, or years) over which the frequency, volume, and intensity of training are systematically varied to avoid overtraining and to promote continued progress.

cycling—Systematically changing the frequency, volume, and intensity of training.

dumbbell—A piece of weight training equipment, typically used in single-arm exercises, that consists of a short bar with weight plates on each end.

dynamic—Exercise involving movement; its opposite is static.

dynamic muscle action—Involves movement and consists of concentric, eccentric, or both types of muscle activity.

eccentric muscular action—A muscular action in which there is tension in the muscle. However, the muscle lengthens rather than shortens. An example can be seen in the lowering phase of the biceps curl, where the biceps muscles are lengthening even

though there is tension in the muscle. Eccentric muscle actions are associated with the muscle soreness commonly experienced in weight training.

ergogenic aid—A substance used to enhance performance.

essential fat—The fat stored in the marrow of the bones as well as in the heart, lungs, liver, spleen, kidneys, muscles, and lipid-rich tissues throughout the central nervous system. A minimum value of 3 percent for males and 12 percent in females is required for normal physiological functioning.

exercise prescription—An exercise program based on present fitness levels and desired goals or outcomes.

extension—A movement occurring at a joint that increases the angle of the joint. The downward movement of the triceps press-down is an example of elbow extension.

fast-twitch fiber—A type of skeletal muscle fiber that is highly recruited during explosive muscular activities (e.g., sprinting, shot putting, and competitive weightlifting).

fat—Essentially nonmetabolically active tissue that contains approximately 9 kilocalories per gram and should constitute 25 to 30 percent of the diet.

fixed resistance machine—A weight training machine in which the location of the weight stack does not move resulting in an inconsistent load during exercise.

flexibility—The ability of a joint to move through its available range of motion.

flexion—A movement occurring at a joint that decreases the angle of the joint. The upward movement of the biceps curl is an example of elbow flexion.

free weight—An object such as a barbell or dumbbell used for physical conditioning and competitive lifting.

frequency—The number of training sessions in a given time period, for example three times a week.

hand off—An assist by the spotter in moving the bar off the supports for the lifter.

hormone—A chemical substance secreted by an endocrine gland that has a specific effect on activities of other cells, tissues, and organs.

hydrostatic weighing—A method of body composition determination utilizing underwater weighing and calculation of body volume and density. Generally accepted as one of the most accurate methods of determining body composition.

hyperplasia—An increase in muscle size due to muscle fibers splitting and forming separate fibers. Experts agree that hyperplasia occurs in animals, but do not agree that it occurs in humans.

hypertension—High blood pressure. Systolic blood pressure over 140 mmHg or diastolic blood pressure over 90 mmHg.

hypertrophy—A term used to describe an increase in the cross-sectional area of the muscle. More simply stated, an increase in muscle size.

hyperventilation—Excessive ventilation of the lungs due to increased depth and frequency of breathing, usually resulting in the elimination of carbon dioxide. Accompanying symptoms include low blood pressure, dizziness, and rapid breathing.

intensity—The relative stress level that the exercise stimulus places on the appropriate system.

ischemia—A condition in which there is reduced supply of oxygen to working tissues.

isokinetic—A type of muscular activity in which contractions occur at a constant velocity as controlled by an ergometer. The term can only describe a concentric muscle action.

isometric (or static) contraction—A type of muscular activity in which there is tension in the muscle but it does not shorten. The bony attachments are fixed or the forces functioning to lengthen the muscle are countered by forces that are equal to or greater than those generated by the muscle to shorten.

isotonic—Implies a dynamic event in which the muscle generates the same amount of force through the entire movement. Such a condition occurs infrequently, if at all, in human performance. Therefore, it is proposed that the term should not be employed to describe human exercise performance. In loose terms, however, it is used to describe dynamic free weight exercises and some machine exercises.

kilocalorie (Kcal)—A unit of work or energy equal to the amount of heat required to raise the temperature of 1 kilogram of water 1 degree Celsius. A quantity of energy equal to 1,000 calories.

lean body weight—Body weight minus fat weight; non-fat or fat-free weight.

ligament—Dense connective tissue that attaches the articulating surfaces of bones together.

load—Total amount of weight lifted.

locks—On barbells or dumbbells, these are located on the outside of the collars and serve to hold the plates (weights) on the bar.

metabolism—The sum total of the chemical changes or reactions occurring in the body.

motor unit—An individual motor nerve and all the muscle fibers it innervates (stimulates).

movement pattern—The line of travel of the body and the bar or equipment during a repetition.

multiple sets—Performing more than one set of an exercise (after a rest period) before moving to another.

multipurpose machine—A training apparatus that has several exercise stations.

"muscle bound"—A term that has been used to link individuals who weight train with limited joint flexibility. This reduced flexibility can be due to a lack of muscle activity or to chronic use of poor lifting and stretching methods. The term is inappropriate for those who practice sound weight training techniques and proper stretching exercises.

muscular endurance—The capacity of a muscle to repeatedly contract over a period of time without undue fatigue. This is a local muscle characteristic.

muscular strength—The capacity of a muscle to exert maximally once. This is a local muscle characteristic oftentimes expressed as the 1RM.

Nautilus—A brand of dynamic resistance training equipment.

"negative" exercise—A form of exercise, more appropriately termed eccentric exercise, in which the muscle lengthens rather than shortens.

neuromuscular—Jointly involving the nervous and the muscular system.

nutrition—The study of food and how the body uses it. The sum total of the processes involved in taking in food and the subsequent metabolic effects.

Olympic bar—It is approximately 7 feet in length and has rotating sleeves on the ends to hold the weights. The diameter of the bar is about 1 inch in the middle and 2 inches at the ends. Its weight is 45 pounds; with Olympic locks it typically weighs 55 pounds.

Olympic weightlifting—A form of competitive lifting that involves contesting maximum strength levels in the clean and jerk and the snatch.

one-repetition maximum (1RM)—The resistance (load) at which the individual can perform only 1 repetition using a maximum effort.

open grip—A hand position, sometimes referred to as a false grip, in which the thumbs are not wrapped around the bar.

overhand grip—The hands grip the bar so that the palms are pronated (face down) and/or away.

overload principle—Progressively increasing the intensity or volume of workouts over the course of a training program as exercise tolerance improves.

overtraining—A state of undue mental and/or physical fatigue brought about by excessive training without sufficient rest.

oxygen uptake—The ability of the heart and lungs to take in and utilize oxygen. Commonly expressed in milliliters of oxygen per kilogram of body weight per minute ($ml \cdot kg^{-1} \cdot min^{-1}$).

percent body fat—The percentage of body weight that is comprised of fat. The ratio of fat to fat-free weight. Recommended ranges are 14 to 18 percent for men and 22 to 26 percent for women.

physical fitness—A product of a high level of cardiorespiratory endurance, muscular strength, muscular endurance, and flexibility and a low ratio of body fat to lean body weight.

power lifting—A competitive sport that involves contesting strength levels in the back squat, bench press, and deadlift exercises.

progressive resistance—Gradually increasing the load (intensity) over time to bring about desired improvements.

pronated grip—Grasping the bar so the palms face down, and the thumbs face each other. Also termed an overhand grip.

prone—Lying face downward; the opposite of supine.

progressive overload—Introducing overloads in a systematic manner.

protein—A food substance, containing approximately 4 kilocalories per gram, that provides the amino acids essential for the growth and repair of tissue.

pyramid training—A method of multi-set training in which loads get progressively heavier or lighter.

quick-lift exercise—A weight training exercise characterized by explosive movements; examples include the power clean, snatch, and hang clean.

range of motion (ROM)—The available movement through which a body part rotates about a joint.

recruitment—The activation of motor units by the neuromuscular system during muscular activity.

relative strength—A comparative measure of strength based upon some variable such as total body weight or lean body weight.

repetition—The execution of an exercise one time.

repetition maximum (RM)—The maximum load that a muscle group can lift over a given number of repetitions before fatiguing. For example, a 10RM load is the *maximal* load that can be lifted for 10 repetitions.

resistance training—Any method or form of exercise requiring one to exert force against resistance.

rest interval—A given amount of time for the pause between sets or exercises.

set—In weight training, the number of repetitions consecutively performed in an exercise without resting.

skeletal muscle—A type of muscle tissue attached to the bone via tendon that respond to voluntary stimulation from the brain.

slow-twitch fiber—A type of skeletal muscle fiber that has the ability to repeatedly work without undue fatigue. This type of muscle fiber is highly recruited for long-distance running, swimming, and cycling events.

smooth muscle—A type of involuntary muscle tissue located in the eyes and in the walls of the stomach, intestines, bladder, uterus, and blood vessels.

specificity of training—The idea that one should train in a specific manner for a specific outcome.

split system (split routine)—A weight training program characterized by certain exercises (for example, upper body exercises and lower body exercises) being performed on alternate days.

squat rack—Standards used to hold a barbell at shoulder height; typically used in placing the bar on the back for the squat exercise.

standard bar—A bar used for weight training that is 1 inch in diameter and typically weighs approximately 5 pounds per foot.

static stretch—Involves holding a static position, passively placing the muscles and connective tissues on stretch.

sticking point—The point in the range of motion of an exercise that is the most difficult to move the weight or resistance through.

strength plateau—A temporary leveling off of progress in a strength training program.

strength training—The use of resistance methods to increase one's ability to exert or resist force for the purpose of improving performance. The training may utilize free weights, the individual's own body weight, machines, or other devices to attain this goal.

striated muscle—Skeletal muscle possessing alternate light and dark bands, or striations. Except for the cardiac muscle, all striated muscles are voluntary.

super set—Consecutively performing two exercises that train opposing muscle groups without rest between them.

supinated grip—Grasping the bar so the palms face upward or away and thumbs are in opposite directions. Also termed an underhand grip.

supine—Lying on the back, facing upward; the opposite of prone.

supplemental exercise—Exercises used in addition to main or core exercises to intensify the training of a certain muscle or muscle group. Sometimes referred to as assistance or noncore exercises.

tendon—Dense connective tissue that attaches a muscle to a bone.

testosterone—A hormone responsible for male sex characteristics.

underhand grip—The hands grip the bar so that the palms face upward (supinated) while the thumbs face away from each other.

underwater weighing—A technique utilized to determine body density. Knowing the density of the body, the percentage of body fat can be calculated. Also termed hydrostatic weighing.

Universal—A brand of dynamic resistance equipment.

variable resistance machine—A weight machine in which the location of the weight stack varies to create a more consistent load during exercises.

variation—Manipulating the frequency, intensity, duration, and/or mode of an exercise program to promote maximal improvements with minimal opportunities for overtraining (both mental and physical).

vitamin—An organic material that acts as a catalyst for vital chemical (metabolic) reactions.

volume—The total work load per exercise, per session, per week, etc. In weight training, the volume is proportional to the total number of repetitions times the total amount of weight. Sometimes volume is defined as sets times the number of reps.

warm-up—A period in which an individual performs light or mild exercise immediately before a training session. The primary purpose of the warm-up is to prepare the body for more intense exercise.

weight training—Exercises performed using free weights, machines, or other forms of resistance for the purpose of increasing strength, muscular endurance, and/or muscle size.

REFERENCES

Baechle, T.R. (Ed.). (1994). *Essentials of strength and conditioning.* National Strength and Conditioning Association. Champaign, IL: Human Kinetics.

Baechle, T.R., & Conroy, B.P. (1990). Preseason Strength Training. In M. Mellion, M. Walsh, & G. Shelton (Eds.), *Team physician's handbook* (pp. 34-40) (2nd ed.). New York: Hanley and Belfur.

Baechle, T.R., & Earle, R.W. (1995). *Fitness weight training.* Champaign, IL: Human Kinetics.

Baechle, T.R., & Groves, B.R. (1994). *Weight training instruction: Steps to success.* Champaign, IL: Human Kinetics.

Baechle, T.R., & Groves, B.R. (1994). *Weight training steps to success video.* Champaign, IL: Human Kinetics.

Clark, N. (1997). *Nancy Clark's sports nutrition guidebook.* (2nd ed.) Champaign, IL: Human Kinetics.

Corbin, C., & Lindsey, R. (1997). *Concepts of physical fitness with laboratories* (9th ed.). Dubuque, IA: Brown.

Fleck, S.J., & Kraemer, W.J. (1997). *Designing resistance training programs.* (2nd ed.) Champaign, IL: Human Kinetics.

Garhammer, J. (1986). *Sports Illustrated strength training.* New York: Harper & Row.

Hoeger, W.K. (1995). *Lifetime fitness, physical fitness, and wellness* (4th ed.). Englewood, CO: Morton.

Komi, P.V. (1992). *Strength and power in sport.* Champaign, IL: Human Kinetics.

Kraemer, W.J., & Baechle, T.R. (1989). Development of a strength training program. In J. Ryan & F.L. Allman, Jr. (Eds.), *Sports medicine* (pp. 113-127) (2nd ed.). San Diego, CA: Academic Press.

Lombardi, V.P. (1989). *Beginning weight training: The safe and effective way.* Dubuque, IA: Brown.

Sprague, K. (1996). *More muscle.* Champaign, IL: Human Kinetics.

Stone, M.H. (1993). *Position statement on anabolic-androgenic steroid use by athletes.* Colorado Springs, CO: National Strength and Conditioning Association.

Westcott, W. L. (1996). *Building strength and stamina.* Champaign, IL: Human Kinetics.

Westcott, W.L., & Baechle, T.R. (1998). *Strength training past 50.* Champaign, IL: Human Kinetics.

ABOUT THE AUTHORS

Thomas R. Baechle, EdD, CSCS, NSCA-CPT, is the executive director of the NSCA Certification Commission, the certifying body for the National Strength and Conditioning Association (NSCA), and is president of the National Organization for Competency Assurance (NOCA), an international organization that sets quality standards for credentialing organizations. He is cofounder, past president, and former director of education for the NSCA, and in 1985 was named its Strength and Conditioning Professional of the Year.

For 20 years Dr. Baechle competed successfully in Olympic-style weightlifting and powerlifting, setting various Midwest records, and for more than 20 years he coached collegiate powerlifting teams and taught weight training classes. He has authored or edited six weight training books, including NSCA's comprehensive *Essentials of Strength Training and Conditioning* and the highly popular *Fitness Weight Training*. He currently serves as chair of the department of exercise science at Creighton

Thomas R. Baechle

University, where he has received several honors, including an Excellence in Teaching Award.

Dr. Baechle holds certifications as a Level I weightlifting coach (United States Weightlifting Federation), a Strength and Conditioning Specialist and Personal Trainer (NSCA), and an Exercise Test Technologist and Exercise Specialist (American College of Sports Medicine [ACSM]). A member of NSCA, ACSM, and the American Alliance for Health, Physical Education, Recreation and Dance (AAHPERD), he has served on the board of directors for the American Heart Association (state affiliate), AAHPERD (state and district), NSCA, and NOCA.

He lives in Omaha, Nebraska, with his wife Susan and two sons, Todd and Clark, He enjoys woodworking and making crafts.

Barney R. Groves

Barney R. Groves, PhD, CSCS, started competing in powerlifting at age 55 and has since won state and regional championships. In 1994, he placed second in a national meet in the 50 and older age group. With more than 25 years' experience teaching weight training, Dr. Groves is a professor of physical education at Virginia Commonwealth University, where he has also served as a strength and conditioning coach and weight training instructor.

Dr. Groves received his doctoral degree in physical education from Florida State University. A member of ACSM and NSCA, he is certified as a Strength and Conditioning Specialist by NSCA and as a Health/Fitness Instructor by ACSM. He is also a former president of the Virginia Association of Health, Physical Education, Recreation, and Dance and has received that organization's 15 year Honor Award for Outstanding Service to the Profession.

Dr. Groves and his wife Patsy live in New Kent, Virginia, where his pastimes include flying as a private pilot and raising 50 head of cattle.

Other resources from Thomas Baechle and Human Kinetics

This video uses slow motion, freeze frames, and graphics to demonstrate the proper positioning and lifting techniques for each exercise. It also gives tips on choosing the right equipment and presents programs for free weights, single- or multi-station pivot machines, and cam machines.

1993 • Item MBAE0243 • ISBN 0-87322-485-X
$29.95 ($44.95 Canadian)

Six color-coded workout zones containing 50 progressive workouts let you choose your own pace and type of result—muscle toning, body shaping, or strength development. Sample weight training programs show you how to organize the workouts into a safe, effective training plan.

1995 • Paper • 176 pp • Item PBAE0445 • ISBN 0-87322-445-0
$15.95 ($21.95 Canadian)

Thirty-five leading thinkers in exercise science explore the scientific principles, concepts, and theories as well as the practical how-tos of strength training and conditioning. Up-to-date, comprehensive information on the structure and function of body systems, training adaptations, testing and evaluation, exercise program design, and organization and administration of the training facility.

1994 • Cloth • 560 pp • Item BNSC0694 • ISBN 0-87322-694-1
$49.00 ($72.95 Canadian)

Wayne Westcott and Tom Baechle, world-renowned experts, show the most effective way for mature adults to work their muscles. Includes strength tests; 9 safety essentials; 39 age-appropriate exercises; a 10-week workout plan; and personalized programs.

1998 • Paper • 240 pp • Item PWES0716 • ISBN 0-88011-716-8
$16.95 ($24.95 Canadian)

Prices subject to change

HUMAN KINETICS
The Premier Publisher for Sports & Fitness
http://www.humankinetics.com/
2335

To place your order, U.S. customers
call TOLL FREE 1-800-747-4457.
Customers outside the U.S. place your order using the appropriate telephone number/address shown in the front of this book.

More books for strength trainers

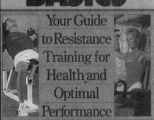